*For Frank McTeague and Bill Moore,
English Coordinators, who were our mentors
many years ago and set us on the path.*

David Booth, Joan Green, Jack Booth

I Want To Read!

Reading, Writing, & Really Learning

 Ontario Institute for Studies in Education/University of Toronto

David Booth

We are grateful to the educators and administrators who provided their insights and expertise in our profiles of teacher and student experiences. We are indebted to Teresa Carleton for her judicious and precise revisions of the text and Larry Swartz, Masayuki Hachiya, and Jay Booth for their contributions to the production of the manuscript.

The dedication and skill of the editorial and production team at Rubicon Publishing, Inc. made our task much easier. We are grateful.

We would like to acknowledge Pembroke Publishers for permission to use references from *The Literacy Principal*; *Reading, Writing in the Middle Years*; and *Even Hockey Players Read*.

 © 2004 Rubicon Publishing Inc.
www.rubiconpublishing.com

Published by Rubicon Publishing Inc. in association with Harcourt Canada

www.harcourtcanada.com

Editor: Teresa Carleton
Art/Creative Director: Jennifer Drew-Tremblay
Designer: Rhonda Ridgway

Library and Archives Canada Cataloguing in Publication

Booth, David
    I want to read : Reading, Writing & Really Learning / David Booth, Joan Green, Jack Booth.

ISBN 1-897096-67-4

    1. English language—Study and teaching. 2. Literacy. I. Green, Joan
II. Booth, Jack, 1946- III. Title.

LC149.B66 2004   428'.0071   C2004-904730-2

I Want To Read!

Reading, Writing, & Really Learning

David Booth • Joan Green
Jack Booth

Rubicon

LEARNING
THROUGH
LITERACY

About the Authors

David Booth is a renowned educator and professor emeritus in the Curriculum, Teaching and Learning Department at OISE/UT. As a classroom teacher, consultant, speaker, and writer, he has delighted thousands with his energy, enthusiasm, and commitment. He is well known as an international speaker, having worked with teachers and administrators throughout Canada, the United States, Great Britain, Australia, and Asia. He is the author of dozens of books for teachers, educators, and parents.

Joan Green has had a distinguished career as an educator and leader in the public sector. She served as the Director of Education for the Toronto Board of Education from 1990 - 1995. In 1995, Joan became the founding CEO of the Ontario Education Quality and Accountability Office (EQAO). In 2002, she was appointed a Commissioner on Education for the Province of Alberta. Joan is a published author on curriculum, assessment, leadership, and equity issues. She has received many honours and awards, including the Distinguished Educator Award from OISE/UT. Currently the Chair of the board of Roots of Empathy, Joan has been a member of the board for hospital, university, and cultural institutions.

Jack Booth has been involved in the educational community for over 30 years. He has taught elementary grades, served as a resource teacher for grades 7-10, and was an English/Language Arts consultant for grades K-12. Recently, Jack has been an educational development author/consultant for publishers in Canada and China. Jack is the author of numerous professional development materials and resources for students. Jack has presented lectures, workshops, and seminars across North America, the United Kingdom, and Asia.

CONTENTS

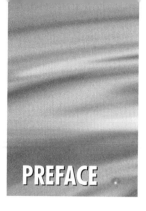

PREFACE

In this book, we take a careful look at the teaching of reading and writing in our schools today, and the implications for literacy learning for all of our students — from youngsters who are just beginning school, to adolescents who are moving on. How can we prepare our students working in classrooms today for the demands of a constantly evolving technical world? What role does parenting play in developing independent readers and writers? What expectations is society placing on the literacy capabilities of our graduates? Today, we are observing differences in how and what many boys and girls read, and we have a large second-language population who may require more time and resources for reaching success in English. We have many students who are already engaged in meaningful literacy activities and who need encouragement to go the full distance. And what of the tens of thousands of young people who have fallen behind their peers in becoming strong readers and writers? What school and community plans do we need to devise in order to encourage and support these dependent learners? How should schools be organized so that teachers can help students develop as proficient readers and writers participating in a wide variety of literacy contexts?

Throughout *I Want to Read*, you will find real classroom moments provided by teachers who are directly and deeply involved with literacy teaching and learning — educators reflecting on the insights they have gained through working with their students. We have included case studies and profiles of students, and schools, that capture the lessons learned by both teachers and students about becoming print powerful. These classroom anecdotes can help to illuminate both the philosophical and the practical premises that underpin a vibrant literacy classroom.

Encouraging young people to become effective, critical, and appreciative readers and writers with a variety of texts and media must be one of the central goals of any school that cares about its students in today's pluralistic communities. We need teachers, schools, and districts that work in concert toward a philosophy and a system of supporting learning through literacy inside and across every curriculum area, for every student.

A myriad of change has occurred in literacy education over the last fifty years. We ourselves have been involved in decades of designing and delivering curriculum guides, literacy programs, and assessment guides. We can't even count the educational initiatives in which all of us have participated in the name of helping our youngsters learn: the institutes, workshops, courses, speeches, in-service sessions, and books written. We have amassed books, articles, and e-files full of techniques, strategies, programs, and stories, chronicling our history of thinking about ways to help all of our students become confident language users in all the contexts in which their lives place them.

But one factor remains constant — every weekday morning, the students arrive at the school's doorstep, waiting (and sometimes even wanting) to enter. We celebrate good schools and those teachers who have grown professionally through the years of change and reflection, no matter which labels we use to describe our programs. And we need to state up front that we welcome the evolution of promising practice — but how sweet it is to see, in each new educational movement, those teaching and learning events that remain significant staples of all powerful literacy classrooms.

In the end, no one knows the students' capacities, or is in a position to construct the way forward for learners, better than the classroom teacher. Excellence is never an accident — it results from high expectations, deep commitment, intelligent direction, and skilful teaching. Excellence represents wise choices among many alternatives, requires shared responsibility, and galvanizes school-wide change to meet our students' literacy needs.

We have strong and heartfelt convictions about what students have to know, do, and value to become engaged readers and writers. Teachers, parents, school leaders, and community members must work steadfastly together to ensure opportunity and optimism for all our students in order to foster a literate citizenry.

We can't afford to get it wrong.

– David Booth, Joan Green, Jack Booth

CHAPTER 1

The New Literacies: Reading the Page, Reading the Screen

Never being much of a book person myself I didn't want to do the book report, because I had never liked any type of reading and had no idea as to what book to read until my teacher suggested Monster, *a book about a 17-year-old named Steven, who had been into trouble with the law. ...*

Before even opening the book, I thought that I might be able to relate, but the only problem was that I am a very slow reader and I only had four days to complete my report on Monster. *I asked Mrs. O'Brien if there was a tape of the book that I might be able to listen to because I did not have any faith that I would be able to finish this book on time if I did it independently. She was nice enough to take me to our school library and get the tape for me. I knew I would be able to finish the book in time if I had someone read it to me and I could just read along, but I was so worried that I wouldn't finish in time. I had such a poor attitude to reading. I brought the tape home and played it while following the words along in the book. What interested me about the novel was that Steve was a lot like me. He, too, got caught up with the wrong crowd... I could relate to what Steve was going through. ...*

My feelings about the book were amazing... I don't normally like reading, but I found a book that I could relate to and that made the time fly by. ...

When I arrived at the ending of the book, I felt that I had learned so much about myself. ... Monster *helped me realize that I can do anything I put my mind to, and if it wasn't for my teacher helping push me, I would never have finished my book and passed that class, and changed my life.*

- Carlton
12th Grade, Special Reading Class

Language, Learning, and Literacy

Today, we have tens of thousands of books, journals, e-files, and research documents that attempt to provide background in how we should teach reading and writing. And yet, for many children and adolescents, becoming effective readers and writers can be a difficult, even painful, process.

Researchers have given teachers an awareness of how children develop intellectually and how they find meaning in everything and everyone around them. Ethnographic studies have alerted us to the social context of learning and the importance of a child's home culture. We now recognize the importance of teachers establishing links with the child's home — both in order to learn about children from their parents, and to allow parents to be partners with the school in helping their children become readers and writers.

Our attitudes to the teaching of reading and writing have altered. Educational writers question traditional practice based on their own observations and research. We need to be aware of some of our subjective assumptions about language and literacy — what we know as English may not be English at all to a child for whom English is a second language (ESL) or dialect (ESD). Even within what we call "Standard" English, society's many groups develop special words to communicate common interests, such as the jargon used by engineers, sports fans, and even teachers; and different generations use words and idioms in diverse ways. A further complicating factor for teachers is that many children come from homes where the language of the classroom is not spoken, either in the vocabulary used or the style chosen. Yet the need to communicate is common to all. We become active members of society through our use of language; we represent and negotiate our thoughts through the different functions of the language (or languages) we speak. We learn how language works — the rules

> *Human beings differ from chimpanzees in having complex, grammatical language. But language does not spring fully formed from the brain; it must be learned from other language-speaking human beings. This capacity to learn is written into the human brain by genes that open and close a critical window during which learning takes place. One of those genes, FoxP2, has recently been discovered on human chromosome 7 by Anthony Monaco and his colleagues at the Wellcome Trust Centre for Human Genetics in Oxford. Just having the FoxP2 gene, though, is not enough. If a child is not exposed to a lot of spoken language during the critical learning period, he or she will always struggle with speech.*
>
> *Matt Ridley*
> *TIME*
> *2 June 2003*

that govern its use — as we struggle to be heard and understood. It is as an instrument of social interaction that children acquire language. They need it to communicate, to participate in society.

Human beings learn to speak without formal instruction. Even as babies, we make talk-like sounds when other people are talking, using language to learn, and learning to use language at the same time. If we are surrounded by people who use words to tell stories, express feelings, convey ideas, and ask questions, and who expect the same of us, we will give shape to our experiences through language. By building on this understanding and working with their interests and abilities, a teacher can motivate students to extend their use of language and their knowledge about language. The school can provide a sense of community that comes from participating naturally in activities that incorporate the functions of language.

When the focus is on using the many functions of language for real purposes, literacy skills will grow across the whole curriculum.

The needs of students as language learners are recognized when literacy is taught with real occasions for using language, rather than through "practice runs." When the focus is on using the many functions of language for real purposes, literacy skills will grow across the whole curriculum. When students are interested in what they are hearing, reading, or writing, they can develop control over the medium of language, as well as explore the context of each experience. In other words, students need to find themselves in situations that require real language for real communicating.

Students become literate not by giving the expected answers to formula questions, but by risking, attempting, failing, responding, and inventing inside the language frame. The way in which those around them respond helps shape their literacy development. Students test hypotheses about the way language works as they interact with others in conversation about texts. They learn to control the ways they use language as their understanding of the rules of the system grows. They struggle to find vocabulary with the power to communicate their message. They experiment with the forms of language to make it do what they want it to.

Mary Gordon, Founding President of Roots of Empathy, asked the question, "Now that public schools have the brain research on the early years, what are they going to do about it?"

Recent studies in the field of neuroscience reinforce the critical importance of the first three years of a child's life. It is during this critical period that a child develops competence and coping skills which establish their future trajectory for success or failure. …

The plasticity of the brain in the first three years makes it vital to support parents as they provide the environment in which their child's brain is being wired. It is therefore imperative that the education system becomes involved with parents during this time, rather than only at the time of school entrance. …

Public schools need to shift their thinking and broaden their mandate to include universal parenting education and child development programs for families with young children aged 0 - 4. These should include a rich play-based, child development program for the children, and opportunities for the parents to learn how to support optimal development of their children. … (Mary Gordon)

What is more, research tells us that home practices greatly affect school practices.

Case Study of a Meaning-maker

Oliver loves playing The Sims and other video games at home. What he enjoys most about video games is engaging with the characters. In particular, with The Sims, he gets into the mind of the protagonists and matches them up accordingly. If he could, he would come home from school, turn on the computer, play The Sims, and then go to bed; and when he got home from school the next day, the cycle would begin again. In *What Video Games Have to Teach Us About Learning and Literacy*, James Gee analyzes the effect video games have on our children's learning and literacy development. Video games like The Sims, in which you control the trajectory of a story by choosing specific characters with singular traits and dispositions and the premise of the story line, have an impact on how children learn. Gee speaks of video games as "… a new form of art. They will not replace books; they will sit beside them, interact with them, and change by the choices people make in the networks of interlocking options of semiotic resources." How well does Oliver do in language activities in school? Moderately well, and he is moderately interested.

And if his program moved in the direction of his personal set of language skills, he could do so much better.

The Texts of Our Lives

Preliterate behaviour often occurs outside of school — in the home or in daycare, or at the park. In terms of literacy teaching and learning, there is an inextricable tie between home and school. We need to contemporize our perspective on the home-school tie to match shifts in our modern media, and in the types of texts (print, electronic, and video) our students are using.

We actively engage with printed forms, but always with a look to context. Where and how do students use texts? How do these practices differ at home versus at school? Why do boys seem to naturally gravitate to non-fiction, and broadly speaking, fact-based texts, where girls opt for fiction? We therefore cross a vast terrain of important work in the area of preliteracy. We touch on each of these issues to make a call for change in the way we regard, and indeed teach, literacy. We need to understand the principles through which our children become literate.

When families of all types interact day-to-day, there is extensive language used — whether it be over a meal, working on homework, going over or writing lists, reading from documents, or reading the local newspaper. We are always and everywhere using language as our vehicle of expression in our communities of practice.

We need to understand that literacy is not only about decoding and encoding words, but instead it is about communicating in a variety of ways in different contexts. With new forms of communication emerging every day, our curricula and programs need to speak to the web of language needs our students require as they text-message friends, write code for a website, or engage with blogs, among other activities. Most literacy curricula and programs do not account for these new identities and their connected texts, and frequently do not assume the sophistication of skills that our students possess. Even in the preschool years, children should be exposed to the intentionality of print, story structure, and linguistic register of written language.

In this model of literacy development, language can only be understood in a specific context within institutions, communities, workplaces, and other social fields — all of which have differing, and at times, overtly conflicting patterns, values, language ideologies, and rules of exchange. School-based literacy becomes, then, one of the many literacies that individuals and/or groups may develop and use. Many young people struggle with the texts of school, especially the print texts they are required to read. How can we engage them and support them in their literacy learning?

There are three core components of a more multi-faceted approach to literacy development: text, context, and identity. By **text**, we are referring to the different "texts" our students use — the Web, cartoons and comics, magazines, newspapers, and graphic novels. Our language programs can and must include texts — print and electronic — of all kinds if our students are to:

- retain interest in growing as readers and writers;
- invest in their literacy activities;
- demonstrate achievement in their literacy learning.

By building lesson plans around both modern and more traditional texts, we provide students with more space to pursue their language understandings and interest.

Text, context, and identity

Next comes the role of **context**. Just as each school is different by virtue of community, administration, and teachers, so too, is each classroom unique. It can be made up of students from diverse backgrounds with different value systems. These conditions of students' lives play key roles in how we will need to create literacy programs that connect home literacy and school literacy.

Our students carry different ideas about language learning and as literacy educators, we need to remember that their understandings do not solely rest on school's model of literacy. Many of our students have studied in other countries, or have even learned English in very different pedagogical frameworks. These frameworks and approaches to language continue to inform the way they will experience literacy. Our students do not learn in a vacuum, either at home or in school. We have to build on the contexts of our students' lives in the literacy programs we develop.

The final ingredient in any literacy event is **identity**. Each student has particular interests and literacy strengths. Although we cannot build our programs around 25 different personalities, we can certainly take into account the unique identities of the children in classrooms by opening up our programs to various types of texts and activities that consider the students' different approaches to learning. Through program components such as independent reading, the writing process, grouping for novel study, and literature circles, we promote, value, and support the differences our students bring to the context of the classroom community.

Preschool Texts

In recent years, educational writers have highlighted the importance of looking outside of schooling in order to solve some of the problems within schooling. We are not suggesting that we transform all the ways in which we teach children to read and write; nor are we asking teachers or parents to abandon all of the valuable pedagogical expertise gained over the past few decades. Rather, our message is that we need to examine contemporary texts and promising practices, so that we can be sure they meet the needs of today's students. This can help us revise our thinking about the reading and writing processes, and our interpretation of what a "text" is. Texts such as basal readers, novels, curriculum resources, and animated stories are artifacts that carry with them assumptions about the reader, about the way they will be read, about the gender of the reader, and even the types of messages that schools promote.

As an institution, a school brings a disparate group of children into one unified space. It is precisely for this reason that we call the early years of childhood preschool. In preschool, children are more frequently left to their own devices, their own cultures, their own routines, and their own speech communities. Then they arrive at school for the first day, where they are inducted into a common culture and a common set of routines. In the outside world, they continue to play video games, read comics, and watch videos. As much as school standardizes, it equally invites different interpretations from each student. Given the multiplicity of needs, it is hardly surprising that literacy is such a complex process, because there are so many literacy strengths and areas to be developed by every student in each classroom.

The preschool years are formative, and all research shows that children gain most learning in the first six years of life. Children carry with them their gender, their cultural heritage, their family narratives and routines, their discursive practices, their home-based texts and practices. All these forces come to bear on how children make meaning in classrooms. Given their role as an equalizer, schools have to inquire constantly about their values, practices, and assumptions in literacy teaching. Schools command the power to transform how and what gets taught to children.

The task of looking critically at literacy and how our young people are taught to read and to write can only be undertaken if we examine present practices in schools and the theories that underpin these practices. Language does not remain a stable system that can simply be taught and learned, so that students are equipped with the skills they require to be future workers. Rather, as Gunther Kress says, in his work *Before Writing*, our literacy curriculum and pedagogy need to be grounded on a theory that treats "individual speakers or writers not as language users but as language makers." We regard youngsters as language makers — deriving literacy from home and school, from texts as diverse as *Thomas the Tank Engine* or *Blues Clues* videos, to video games, interactive websites, and *Maisy* picture books with flaps and full-colour, stylistic illustrations. Our students are not sitting at home lingering over basal readers. They are multimodal readers learning and making language from websites, from videos, and from multimodal texts of all kinds and in every shape and size imaginable. The ascendance of the visual over the written has, of course, had a dramatic impact on the way today's students make meaning.

> *Schools have to inquire constantly about their values, practices, and assumptions in literacy teaching.*

We cannot understand how children find their way into print unless we understand the principles of their meaning-making. In our thinking, subconsciously or unconsciously, in our feelings, we constantly translate from one medium to another. In the new communication and global world, it may well be that these will be essential requirements for culturally, socially, economically, humanly productive and fulfilling lives (Kress).

By looking at children and modern media, changes in literacy learning can be implemented. As Kress notes,

… with the world of popular culture, I think of the "pace" of currently available children's programs on television: rapid fire succession of events, succession of images; rapid editorial cutting from one shot to another, from one segment to another, rapid speech, rapid music. No time here at all for reflection. The image of children and of entertainment implicit in the form of such programs is that of young humans who need to be constantly distracted; who have the attention span of a flea; who will zap to the next channel should the pace slacken for a moment … I also happen to think that the world caught in the "information explosion" — so-called — may need the move to the visual as its new and more effective medium of communication.

Children's television and the surfeit of children's programs are decidedly multimodal: rapid and frequent movements of camera angles in TV shows and movies, and a fusillade of colour and animation in our printed and electronic texts. We have endless varieties and a multiplicity of modes in which to work and ultimately learn and teach.

Reading Everything

Just as the term "literacies" has become plural and refers to any number of bodies of knowledge a person might have, so too has the term "reading" undergone expansion. To "read" an experience is to make meaning of it. Adolescents make meaning through such literacy practices as instant messaging, hypertext documents, videos, computer games, and music. The new technologies and extracurricular literacies are often much better understood and "read" by adolescents than they are by teachers. The institution of school is out of this particular loop and teachers have much to learn from their young students.

The new literacies themselves offer the possibility of a more equitable power balance both in and out of school. People who have traditionally been outside the mainstream now have at least the possibility of access to all kinds of information as well as opportunities to express their views to a wide variety of audiences.

Association for Supervision and Curriculum Development Newsletter, April 2004

> *Reading occurs in every room in the school, in all curriculum areas — and in every aspect of life...*

What took us so long as educators to come to the realization that reading occurs in every room in the school, in all curriculum areas — in science, in math, in social studies, in English/language arts — and in every aspect of life outside school — games, manuals, computers, magazines, newspapers, novels, tax forms, self-help books? When we timetable reading periods, what do we select for students to read as we teach them about literacy? What made us think that one particular novel had to be taught and analyzed, while students in other classrooms were reading entirely different books? Why do some students fail a math test because they can't read or understand the questions? Why are texts chosen by students still not considered literacy resources by many teachers? And why are so many students filling their lives with satisfaction gained from reading and writing outside school, but not inside the classroom? How, then, do we teach reading comprehension, build strong print vocabularies, and enable young writers to construct effective texts that incorporate the standard conventions of print? How can we help students to grow as readers and writers? All of these concerns need to be included in our discussions of literacy programs that will affect today's students.

Literacy Inside and Across the Curriculum

For decades, educators have struggled to make literacy teaching happen "across the curriculum." Students use language to process and negotiate their experiences and construct meaning throughout the day, not just during a period labelled "English" or "language arts." They will need to practise and develop language competencies "inside" each area of the curriculum. Literacy is at the heart of reading, writing, drama, art, history, mathematics, and science. Literacy has occurred when the students can express concepts and describe experiences in any curriculum area.

True learning has occurred when the students can express concepts and describe experiences in any curriculum area in their own words.

We use the term "literacy learning" to encompass not only the theory of language learning, but also to highlight the centrality of language in all aspects of learning. It is shorthand for assumptions, values, and theories not only about what literacy is and how it is learned, used, and taught, but more generally and pervasively, about the essential role of literacy in all curricula and in all learning and teaching.

Literacy learning takes place naturally and continuously as the students approximate, explore, and evaluate. "Subjects" can provide the context for much of the literacy use and growth that occur. Research tells us that instruction and skill development evolve better in meaningful contexts, rather than on practice sheets.

We need to establish programs that help students decipher the unfamiliar and relate it to the patterns of what they already know, and then, often change those patterns. Whether in informative or entertaining contexts, students must see literacy as a useful process. When students are doing more talking, writing, and reading about what matters to them with someone who matters to them, they will be constructing learning more effectively.

A Literacy-based Program

Literacy-based teaching grows out of building the curriculum the way children actually acquire language proficiency — talking, reading, and writing through need and desire. A program based on literacy growth frees the teacher to choose from a range of curriculum options for different students. Learning through literacy can become a metaphor for change, where we question, examine, and reassess our assumptions, reflecting on what we are doing as teachers to promote thoughtful reading and writing. We need to engage in dialogue with one another, observing, coaching, and learning from other teachers, to create a professional community of teachers, just as in our class-rooms we create a community of learners.

We need to make our students feel that reading matters — to us and to them. This may require us to redefine the term "reading" so that all of our students — with different interests, tastes, and abilities — can become members of the literacy club. We can "read" words, images, sounds, movements, and all the combinations thereof. Literacy involves the reader making the most meaning he or she can by negotiating with the interconnecting texts of the reader's world. The multiliteracies depend on the contexts of the reader's life for interpretation. Each of us can "read" a variety of texts depending on our background, facility with the genre or the format, and/or the pragmatics of the situation (for example, if it is a test or a discussion). We need to help youngsters become literate with as many types of "texts" as possible, especially with those we require them to read.

> *Learning through literacy can become a metaphor for change.*

Literature and/or Literacy

How can we help students who are reluctant readers read what society calls "literature"? As teachers, we want our students to be able to interpret and appreciate the books they will experience throughout their lives without setting a frame of boredom or failure.

We don't feel that there is a master list of what everyone should read. We have moved toward supporting a reader's decisions about the print resources he or she selects — newspapers, novels, magazines, work and organizational materials, and what is read for fun and satisfaction. As with films and television, appreciating literature is a developmental, lifelong process, dependent on many variables — personal background, language and thinking processes, life experiences, familiarity with the type of selection, the purpose and payoff of reading, the situation in which the reading is taking place, and especially the readers' attitudes toward texts, often determined by experiences in school. What we can do is open up the options that literary resources offer, and explore with students how different texts work, what to look for and what to expect. In this way, they can be informed in the choices they make, and select the resources that give them the most satisfaction.

In *Will This Be on the Test?* Laura Miller comments on reading lists for secondary students and specifically on what is now called "the classroom classic."

This month, teenagers across the nation, under the orders of their teachers, crack open books that will offer them their first taste of serious critical reading, of puzzling out an author's theme and hunting the wily symbol....

They might read *Frankenstein* or *The Adventures of Huckleberry Finn* ... *The Great Gatsby* — those works they're likely to return to as adults. But they will also ponder novels they'll never forget but also never re-read, a category you could call the classroom classic; it's the kind of book that never seems to shake off that fine layer of chalk dust....

The classroom classic is a literary hazelnut: you crack it open and it easily yields a round, whole meat; that's all there is, no shards or membranes to pick through. You can discuss its theme, but not debate it....

The classroom classic has a clear-cut moral, which is why *Animal Farm* rivals *Lord of the Flies* as the foremost exemplar of the genre....

When we first read them, we understood that being given books with such bleak endings was a compliment to our maturing sensibilities: finally we were ready for the hard stuff....

When *Catcher in the Rye* began to appear on syllabi, a turning point had occurred. By putting the ultimate literary expression of teenage rebellion in their students' hands, teachers were admitting that they no longer worried that kids might read the wrong book. Now we're afraid they'll read no books at all....

The New York Times Book Review
21 September 2003

However, under the headline "Contemporary vs. Classic", Greg Toppo points out that high-school reading has changed with the times.

Faced with declining reading scores on national tests and the steady buzz of movies, TV and video games, teachers trying to entice students are increasingly turning to contemporary literary fiction and non-fiction, often picked fresh from bestseller lists....

"Times have changed — high school has changed," says Niki

Locklear, English department chair at Simon Kenton High School in Independence, Ky. Her seniors just started reading *Tuesdays With Morrie*, the bestselling memoir by sports columnist Mitch Albom.

Teens can learn as much from contemporary literature as from classics, English teachers Amy Crawford and Rick Ayers say in their new guide, *Great Books for High School Kids* (Beacon Press)....

And while it hasn't supplanted *The Scarlet Letter*, Hill says, teachers are assigning books like Dan Brown's 2003 religious-themed thriller *The Da Vinci Code*....

"No one is going to read *The Scarlet Letter* until they're reading something they're enjoying," he says. "You can't hit a home run until you're swinging the bat."

USA Today
24 May 2004

Maybe there are grounds for negotiating our dreams with their realities so that all of us grow in our understanding of each other. Jeannie Wilson, a literacy educator working with teachers and adolescents, confronts the issue of focusing on literacy development or literature appreciation, and supports a teaching construct that includes both approaches in working with readers at risk:

> If we remain open to the possibilities of life, we are immeasurably enriched. Quoyle, the protagonist of Annie Proulx's *The Shipping News*, learns this lesson about love: "... he was wondering if love came in other colours than the basic black of none and the red heat of my obsession." I wonder if the teaching and learning of English comes in other colours than the basic black of literacy and the red heat of my obsession with literature.

If we incorporate popular and contemporary texts that interest young people through the content and style, and if we develop their literacy strategies, they may approach and participate in the reading of a wider variety and complexity of texts. Of course, we must both provide them with highly motivating selections and structure supportive opportunities for reading and discussing them. We want to open and increase the options these students will have for including literature in their lives.

In her remedial reading class for students who were unsuccessful in their exit literacy tests for secondary school, teacher Mary Jo O'Brien does just that. Her room is full of literacy resources, and her students know that she cares about everyone in the room. She fills classrooms with print resources that hook the students. Students select and read these highly motivating texts — magazines, novel, advertisements, stories, and poems — voluntarily, and she is able to incorporate their interests in her teaching of the necessary strategies that they require.

Teachers strive to select the best books for their classroom libraries. They look for materials that face up to contemporary social issues and that draw students to authors and books beyond the popular bestsellers. Classrooms should be full of resources for readers beginning to feel success, interest groups, individuals with particular concerns, gifted students needing enrichment, and those beginning to work in English. The presence of books found in the wider world, included alongside their curriculum materials, helps students to see what they read in school as "real," and reading as a lifelong activity.

Popular Texts

We need to be careful not to establish a negative barrier against the popular culture and media — another "us and them" war — bestsellers, magazines, TV shows, films, CDs, and computer games. If we accept these resources as influential in the lives of young people, we can carefully engage students in looking at them through a critical, but never cynical, lens.

Comics are still preferred reading for many boys, especially for those who are labelled "reluctant readers." Some educators consider comics as sub-literature, but many teachers have used comics in the classroom and achieved remarkable results. Students are able to visualize and construct meaning because of the blend of pictures and text. To many adults (generally males), comics represent an art form with critical attributes just like any other.

Comics and graphic novels

Graphic novels are extremely popular with many young men; experienced and able readers still enjoy them, but as reading tastes and writing styles change, readers may make alternative choices.

Today's students can find in the classics a different life from their own in language, custom, place, time, or circumstance. For some, these differences can make the reading difficult — but independent readers may relish the depth of language and content that make up classics. Often, the media repopularize an old book and breathe new life into it, such as *Lord of the Rings*. On the whole, though, we should tread lightly in pushing these books with struggling readers, recognizing that our goal is literacy within the richest, most meaningful context we can create for students.

Students in difficulty often seek out information books, hoping to find one that speaks of what they know, with minimal text, free of idioms and expressions and subtext, and full of visuals. A large proportion of reluctant or limited readers opt for non-fiction: getting information, figuring out what happens, making crafts, keeping track of things, and helping others.

Ron Jobe, in his book *Info-Kids: How to Use Nonfiction to Turn Reluctant Readers into Enthusiastic Learners*, says that reluctant readers want action, raw humour, familiarity, and complex illustrations; in contrast, teachers prefer elegance of story structure, sophistication of character development, complexity of description, irony and references to other literature. Of course, many students read fictional stories — especially action stories in which what the characters do is usually more important than what they think or feel. These are stories of adventure, horror and ghosts, science fiction, sports, war, and spies. We see these themes continued in the bestsellers most enjoyed by adults. Series books, with their predictable themes and familiar characters, often provide security for less confident and able readers. Readers know that the books will be interesting and accessible, and many readers move on to more substantial reading.

Action stories

Peer groups have their own power in determining what its members will want to read, and adults must recognize this if they hope to influence the reading materials selected by youngsters. By providing books that are similar in theme, yet with strong artistic merit, adults can offer young readers an awareness of other types and genres of texts, thereby increasing their literacy options.

If you walk into a corner store, you will be amazed at the sheer number of magazines, many directed at teens. There is no better marker of the differences in "life" reading and in "school" reading than these. How are we who work in schools supposed to accommodate this print resource, an important literacy factor in so many of our students' literacy lives? Even as a free reading enterprise, some schools have banned magazines from the library. To say this is short-sighted is an obvious understatement. One could even argue that it is negligent when we fail to include the materials we know young readers will choose independently. We need to make connections between the texts of their lives.

Magazines

How Readers Learn

Students are constantly exposed to a wide variety of texts, both in and out of school. As students encounter this array of texts, critical literacy becomes a tool for helping them interpret the messages that are embedded in them, connecting them to their present understanding of what they know, or what they thought they knew, and moving them into unfamiliar territory. Critical literacy encourages them to question the authority of texts and address issues of bias, perspective, and social justice that they may contain. Many readers assume that print materials are automatically true. But, as students learn to view texts critically, they come to recognize that texts are full of the author's viewpoints, and often these need to be examined, even challenged.

Students need to move beyond literal understanding...

With the increasing complexity of the texts in our lives, students need to move beyond literal understanding, and to think deeply about what the texts say and mean. Since the texts were created by individuals and groups, these writers have been influenced by their own contexts in society, the choices, the values, and the authority the writers assume. Students can learn to analyze these positions and come to understand that a text is the author's version of the world. Readers make their own meanings from a particular book, from the viewpoint of their own developing lives. Who they are at a particular stage in life will determine to a great extent how they interact with a particular text.

As teachers, we have all experienced the disappointment that comes from students revealing their boredom or dissatisfaction with what we had felt was a significant resource. Finding appropriate and interesting books for our students is a complicated task, but it is at the centre of our struggle to help them become appreciative readers intent on extending their own knowing. (If only they would enjoy what we told them to enjoy, or like a book because we did!) Backgrounds and abilities differ widely in the students we teach, and we need to help them begin to consider their responses to text, to reflect on why they feel as they do, and to consider the author's role in determining how they responded to a particular selection.

For so many of us, how and what we read today is different from even the nearby past. We choose materials that can be handled easily in short bursts of time; we browse and sample newspapers, professional journals, magazines, websites — smaller snippets of text — and struggle to find time for longer items such as novels and biographies. Many selections are highly visual, filled

Teacher : I'm learning … this is still something I find difficult, especially because so many teachers come to the classroom as readers, English teachers in particular. And the first thing is a sense of disbelief early on, when you realize that not everyone reads what we read, and that for some people, there aren't any wonderful memories around reading experiences. I still struggle with these differences in our lives.

I continue to reflect on the fact that as a competent reader I always have to remember and begin to learn more about those who are not — reflecting on the gap between us. I continue to try to shrink that.

Students have brought magazines into class for independent reading, but I've never actually thought about substituting magazines for books. I could do that if they bring in something that has made a difference or offers a positive reading experience.

Words don't seem to make any sense to one of my students. I know that she resists reading a book because for her it's an exercise in futility. And with kids like that, we share personal stories, and I am beginning to incorporate magazines and other materials. But I still find it difficult. I don't want them to feel any further marginalized in that group. The conversations we've had have been fun and I've learned a great deal about these kids, and I think I've shared a lot with them too — my passion for cars and things like that. I'm feeling as if I'm getting a sense of how to go ahead, how to proceed with really teaching literacy.

with colourful illustrations, detailed drawings and photographs, with a variety of fonts and sizes. Just notice how newspapers have changed their formats and styles for a public that reads differently from readers of the past. Contemporary schooling faces a real dilemma — if we once worried that students didn't know enough, we now must worry that they are overwhelmed with ideas and information at a dizzying rate. Our task is to help them make sense of the vast array of messages they encounter every day.

Young people are bombarded with so much stimuli from television, advertising, and computer games. How will a book full of long, uninterrupted print passages compete with the visual and aural sensations that beat upon them and catch them? Can we use the range of powerful literature that is available today for motivating reluctant readers into exploring the ideas, the other worlds, the information, the surprises, the sense of imagination contained inside the very books they too often disdain? What if these readers could find themselves engaged in a powerful book that they couldn't put down? What would change in their reading lives? Would they forget for the moment their reading difficulties and simply read? Why are some teachers and parents able to find the right books for those youngsters at such a difficult stage in their reading lives? A significant experience with an engaging book can give students something to focus on besides their anxiety over being limited readers.

We can offer students a chance to be emotionally engaged with their print experiences — some for the first time. As well, struggling readers could gain the opportunity to learn how authors use language. The language of literature differs from the language of daily conversations, often offering a richer vocabulary and more complex sentence structure, imagery, and phrasing. We move our students into literature with resources that matter to them and that matter to us.

Special Education interventions using drama and conversation

Children like Alfred who are struggling with reading and writing can benefit greatly from opportunities to play with puppets, interacting creatively to develop language skills by reacting to stories and devising their own scenarios. Also, the focused attention of a volunteer in the classroom working without interruption with a student to explore his or her growing understandings and ideas is invaluable in supporting the breakthrough to independent literacy.

Student: Alfred
Grade or Age: Grade 2
By: Caroline Cremer

Alfred is now seven years old. He is never late, and is rarely away; his homework is consistently done on time. He enjoys group work more than working independently. He lives with his grandmother. His father lives and works in Scarborough and visits him on weekends. Alfred's father tries to be involved in his son's life. He attends parent/teacher interviews and school support team meetings, and sometimes picks Alfred up for lunch. Alfred's mother calls him periodically and, when this occurs, Alfred's behaviour changes. He is generally a happy child though when he hears from his mother, he often appears sad and withdrawn.

Alfred has started going to the Learning Centre every day for half an hour. He still struggles with reading print text, and is currently reading at a beginning grade one level. The books he is able to read independently have predictable word patterns and a natural repetition. He recognizes some high frequency words, but is unable to locate unknown words. He matches word by word while reading a line or more of print and he often uses the pictures to help him read. He is starting to self-correct a few of his errors, though not consistently. Alfred appears to enjoy having stories read to him. He often comments on the pictures and sometimes relates a personal experience to the story. Alfred can also predict what will happen next in the story and can answer some

questions regarding the characters, setting, events and the ending.

One of Alfred's favourite activities is using puppets either to re-enact a story he has heard or to create his own stories, with his own characters, problems and ending. Puppets seem to be the vehicle that demonstrates Alfred's cognitive and oral language skills the best. His creativity, comprehension of familiar texts and understanding of the complexity of issues become most apparent when he works with puppets. Puppets also seem to have a calming effect on Alfred, especially the puppet that one volunteer brings to use to work with him. When the puppets appear, Alfred's attention becomes completely focused; his fidgeting and silliness immediately stop and he becomes engrossed in the puppet.

Alfred requires much help with writing. He struggles with forming his letters and, since grade one, has been seeing the occupational therapist to help develop his fine motor skills. Alfred is easily distracted, and it takes him a long time to complete a few sentences. Talking about his ideas before writing them on paper seems to help him. A volunteer in my class will often sit alone with him and discuss his ideas. The complete attention of one adult is valuable to a child's learning process.

Alfred has recently started writing journal entries on the computer. Although it takes him a while, he seems engaged in the task and motivated to write. Alfred writes about personal topics that are important to him, and is starting to take some risks in spelling.

Often students with special needs are very gifted and capable of in-depth focus

When students' interests and passions are fostered, they bring great enthusiasm and dedication to the learning task. If students are encouraged to examine their own learning and develop metacognitive skills, they can ask for appropriate assistance and take full advantage of the learning opportunities they meet. Sometimes students with special needs do not appear to have learning challenges because they have learned to cope so well with their areas of weakness. They may have critical literacy skills which they apply readily in media or oral contexts. These are strengths on which to build.

Name of Student: Martin
Grade or Age: Grade 11
By: Vida Juozaitis

Martin's passion for *Anime* was boundless. He organized the club viewings faithfully every Friday. Before each viewing, he made tireless efforts to inform me of every detail of the film to ensure I appreciated its aesthetic and thematic value. If nudity or violence was involved, he made doubly sure I was "primed" before the showing and long discussions would take place about the purpose of the naked female figure or the carnage. His bubbly analysis and enthusiasm for the characters, themes, style of animation were illuminating to a novice like me. The range of *Anime* that is available was impressive. He showed *Spirited Away*, which later won the Academy Award, and he made a point of showing films with strong female characters, of which occasionally l got to view a small segment.

Martin consumed everything he could about Japanese *Anime* and Japanese culture. He took out every book in the library on Japan. I began to augment our collection to feed this interest not only for Martin but also for the growing membership, both male and female, in the *Anime Club*. When I began to purchase books about *Manga*, *Anime* and Japan, they would fly out of the library. For his co-op placement, he worked as an assistant chef in a Japanese restaurant, which thrilled him.

Soon after I met Martin, I noticed that sometimes when he was in the library, he was with an educational assistant who scribed for him. I was surprised to discover that Martin had a learning disability. While I realize that many gifted students have learning disabilities, I was still taken aback when he told me in a self-deprecating way that he had difficulty with writing and, to a lesser extent, with reading. As time passed and he became more comfortable with me, he would ask me to assist him in locating resources for his school assignments.

I found Martin to be very determined and quite focused on his academic needs. He was able to articulate very clearly the level of print text he could understand, showing a metacognitive awareness of his comfort reading level.

Marian Hood
Secondary school teacher
Forest Lawn High School
South West Calgary, Alberta

Student population:
1300 students; great cultural diversity.

"I'm in the room with a bunch of people, not with kids. I treat them the way I would treat a respected family member or friend. I treat their writing the way I would treat a colleague's writing."

"No matter how you cut it: you want kids to read, write, listen and speak and be decent human beings on the planet!"

Literacy strategies that work

- tell students stories; ask them to comment on them; elicit questions, which other students answer; retell the stories to determine the effect different perspectives have on the same story;
- read to students frequently; have fifteen minutes of silent free reading at the beginning of every class;
- have students determine what is important in a story as they retell or rewrite it;
- provide boundaries for writing assignments that give guidance, but do not constrain the writer;
- have students extend the characters in a story to a new situation;
- practise writing through extensive free writing — at least fifteen minutes a day;
- use the Internet for resources on high-interest topics;
- use film to teach literary terms; and recognize that film is often students' "text" of choice.

Four things central to the program:
- telling of stories;
- daily writing;
- reading to students;
- visual mapping — to demonstrate kinesthetic intelligence through drawing (focus on detail in graphics, illutrations, tableaux, storyboards etc.).

Assessment:
- comment on and read examples of exemplary student work;
- show students what they do well, and move their skills into other types of text in both reading and writing;
- use rubrics; have students help develop them;
- use a four-point scale to describe excellent and entry level effort, and then ask the students to fill in the middle two categories;
- provide learning tasks on which students will do well;
- read but do not formally evaluate everything that students do.

Other points to consider:
- use networked computers in the classroom;
- use INSPIRATION SOURCE, a mind-mapping program, to encourage and extend writing;
- use HYPERSCORE, freeware developed by PH.D students at MIT, a music creation program for non-musical people that completely reconceptualizes the way music looks; students make up tunes, decide upon the harmony and, where appropriate, write the score and an introduction for others to read;
- collaborate with colleagues to develop ideas and resources to recognize learners' experiences;
- demonstrate a love for reading and writing as a teacher.

Professional Perspectives

CHAPTER 2

The Digital Dividend: Technology and Literacy

The New Literacies

Since literacy is now defined as more than a matter of words on a page, the exploration of "the media" — computers, television, film, magazines, and so on — has been seen as an integral part of the learning continuum. Students of all ages need opportunities to be critical viewers to ensure that they become "media literate." We have to consider the effect of these media and their influence on the thinking, reading, and writing proficiencies of children as we develop our school curriculum. Viewing — the observing process — is an essential component of communication. The technology of the future will bring an ever-increasing flow of visual information, which students will need to learn to comprehend, analyze, and apply to new situations. The critical strategies that we hope to develop in students as they interact with print are just as necessary when they interact with television, film, and communications media brought to us by the computer screen, or technologies yet unknown and undeveloped. Therefore, listening and viewing are vital elements in any literacy program.

> *Students of all ages need opportunities to be critical viewers to ensure that they become "media literate."*

In terms of literacy teaching, our students are not learning to be literate the way we did or even the generation before us did. As Professor Ruth McQuirter Scott said, "As an educator, a writer, and a parent, I struggle to keep up with the dizzying pace of technology. There's a revolution taking place under my nose and trying to understand it is like taking aim at a moving target. I don't dare stand still, since this generation of children will simply move on without me. I'd hate to miss the show!"

Today's students are more savvy about a much broader range of texts, both print and electronic, than we ever were. Their texts have video, animation, hot spots, and, in their world, the written word has been extended by the visual and the tactile. What we need to ask ourselves is, "What kind of dispositions do our children need as they enter school today?" What is clear from looking at modern communication is that our visual landscape has dramatically changed over the past two decades.

In a digital environment, the new literacies our students are developing and expanding involve thinking, exploring, connecting, and making meaning, often collaboratively. Students have the amazing potential of taking advantage of vast global networks, huge databases, immense archives, rich art collections, and interactions with millions of users. As noted earlier, our task as educators is to help young people become capable navigators of what is often a complex and disparate landscape, "making up their own maps and minds" (*Standards for Technological Literacy*).

Many classrooms have already left behind the "teacher as expert" notion where the students are expected to digest, memorize, and regurgitate. We are moving toward classrooms as environments where students living in the Information Age are encouraged to develop flexible and inquiring frames of mind as they sort, sift, weigh, and arrange ideas and construct new concepts. In our complex world where simple answers, basic problem patterns, and memorized solutions are no longer sufficient, students, like all of us, have to shift, change, learn and relearn. The inquiry-based classroom supports the development of a full range of literacies, as students handle the unexpected and the unfamiliar as well as the predicted and the known. Our students must create answers rather than collect them. In an environment filled with opportunities for reading, writing and discussing, students create their own rich web of related questions that help them organize and structure their investigations and develop their emerging understandings.

> *Our students must create answers rather than collect them.*

There are three levels of use of technology that move students in graduated ways along the literacy spectrum. The first order use of technology is the most ubiquitous, where the word processor is used as the electric typewriter, offering little in the way of cognitive scaffolding, but significant efficiencies in production and integration of information. The second order use of technology supports the development of communicative competence, problem solving, inquiry, and informed decision-making — all skills directly linked to the development of literacy. The third order use of technology, less common in our schools and much to be desired, involves knowledge construction, representation and design of ideas, verbally and graphically.

Pat Clifford and Sharon Friesen, of Alberta's Galileo Educational Network, made a very significant observation in this regard: "While we know that many young people spend a lot of time online, we have very little understanding of what kinds of literacy skills they use and need to develop in order to learn effectively in digital environments." They go on to pose two important questions for us to ponder as we plan for the widest and richest literacy learning experiences for students in our classrooms today:

- "Are there ways we can create more engagement with a wider variety of texts so that students are reading for information and pleasure on a more frequent basis? Is there a role for technology in increasing our literacy repertoire in schools?"
- How do we understand reading and composing in hyperlinked and multimedia environments? Or, as educator Andrea di Sessa asks, "Can education be transformed by technology so that children can learn more, learn more easily at an earlier age, and learn with pleasure and commitment? Can we create 'two-way literacies' where everyone becomes a creator as well as a consumer of dynamic and interactive expressive forms?"

> *"Can we create 'two-way literacies' where everyone becomes a creator as well as a consumer of dynamic and interactive expressive forms?"*

As well, Pat Clifford and Sharon Friesen offer an interesting analysis of what they call the three pillars of literacy. The first is the "material pillar," or the signs and symbols of language. We understand that being literate means being able and eager to read a wide range of written materials from comic books, magazines, newspapers, short and long fiction, poetry and non-fiction. We should now be asking: "What is the material basis of digital literacy, and how is it changing what we come to call the basic literacies in a digital age?" The second pillar they speak of is the cognitive one, which addresses how we think. Andrea di Sessa states, "The new computer literacies will build on and extend humans' impressive and dynamic interactive capabilities far more than conventional literacy does." Spatial intelligence is enhanced by the process of writing on and gathering intelligence from websites. Interpersonal connections and personal reflections are fostered by exchanges on email and in chatrooms and discussions forums. Finally, the third pillar of literacy we seek to develop is the social one. In the technological world our learners inhabit, they have diverse opportunities to engage in what Marlene Scardamalia and Carl Bereiter call "knowledge-building": the creation or modification of public knowledge — "knowledge that lives in the world and is available to be worked on and used by other people."

The following newspaper report explores the results and implications of a study involving 150 middle school students who were issued laptop computers for their writing assignments.

> A group of British Columbia students who were armed with laptop computers for their writing assignments increased their English test scores by just over 30 percent, a new study shows....
>
> Just over 90 percent of pupils who were tested met the province's education standards after they started using the laptops. Before they had received laptops, only 70 percent of those pupils met the province's writing standards....
>
> "The technology is putting the joy back into writing," said the principal of technology services. "For a lot of kids, handwriting is an arduous task that they're just not willing to do. The rewriting and improving of their work on the laptops is what they're liking."...
>
> Teachers and parents said the laptop writing program has had a positive impact on the attitudes and confidence of the children involved, particularly boys who were struggling with motivation and attention problems....
>
> The laptops are a hit among the pupils. One thirteen-year-old boy said, "I would always spell things wrong and I would have to redo it. It was always way too messy to read. I liked the laptop a lot. It helped me write better."
>
> *The Globe and Mail,* 14 January 2004
> Caroline Alphonso

We have all witnessed the enthusiasm with which students embrace technology. Information technologies can free students from physical constraints, motivate them, allow them, no matter where they live, to connect with others around the world, provide them with purpose for their projects, and give them access to powerful problem-solving tools. From the simplest talking CD that allows a non-reader to enjoy a story, to the hypermedia software that gives students the power to create their own multimedia presentations, computers are a tool that can empower our students.

The following multimedia poetry collaboration is an illustration of how working with technology can enhance and stimulate learning among grade ten students.

Exhibit #1: Multimedia Poetry Collaboration

PART 1: Students are asked to discuss poetry with parents and adult friends, getting answers to the question: "Is poetry useful?" They then email findings to teachers from home. The findings have to include the range of answers, quotations from poems remembered, and one poem in its entirety that parents mentioned.

PART 2: Students bring a personally selected multimedia image and poem together in order to create "one vivid image" to show the links between poems and images. The students "read" the picture and look for the story implications in it and the connections to the meaning of the poem. In completing these activities, students use web search, cut and paste, graphics editing, converting Word or PowerPoint files to graphics, screen captures and so on.

PART 3: Students are asked to consider a second question: "How do the metre and the metaphor of the poems work together to create the meaning of the poems?" Students enroll in an "online community" to share their creations with other students in other high schools and to talk about the question and the essential components of poetry.

PART 4: Students are asked to think about another question: "How do we construct meaning from images and pictures?" In response to this question, students choose one form of poetry and using this form, create their own poem. After this, they take another multimedia image which is best suited to their poem and merge it with the poem. They also add an "audio" element to the final image. After receiving online "feedback" from each other about their new creations, students revise their work.

PART 5: The students gather in person to present their images and celebrate their work. They make their presentations in a variety of ways — oral readings, audio recordings, readers' theatre, dance and so on.

PART 6: Teachers assess the students' work using:

• rubrics, which appraise students' efforts and quality of work in four areas: online discussion, found poem/image, created poem/image and presentation; and

• a "feedback" form, where students comment on the "pluses" and "minuses" of the project and offer suggestions to improve the project.

(Adapted from *Building New Bridges.* Dr. Michele Jacobsen)

Technology does not necessarily improve the acquisition of literacy in and of itself. It requires carefully crafted learning programs focused on creating dynamic opportunities for the interpretation, manipulation, and creation of ideas in the classroom. The rapid development of the Internet is a little like a gold rush — some miners found earth and not gold.

Literacy needs remain constant with the different media experiences.

We need to help students skim and scan enormous amounts of information, to select and organize what may be useful or significant, to critically examine the information for authenticity and bias. Teachers working with students who are struggling with literacy skills realize that their limitation with print texts often extends to their use of Internet information. Literacy needs remain constant with the different media experiences. There are things we need to be concerned about, ranging from the use of unfiltered, inappropriate materials, to plagiarism, to the need for immediate gratification. Dr. Marilyn Benoit has been a practising child and adolescent psychiatrist for over 25 years. She writes about what she sees as a disturbing trend in children of the "click-generation."

The Dot.com Kids and the Demise of Frustration Tolerance

The problem I see emerging in children is one of decreasing frustration tolerance. In lay language, this translates into a lack of patience, that old-fashioned idea that people of my generation had preached to us repeatedly, "Patience is a virtue."...

The exponential technological advancements of recent years have afforded the possibility for young children to achieve instant gratification at the touch of a button. An 18-month-old can turn on the TV and instantly be entertained by music, dance, interesting shapes and colours, adults, cartoon characters, etc....

Now email and instant messaging have created an expectation of rapid communication. What has ensued is the experience of impatience (poor frustration tolerance) when the response does not come in the anticipated brief turnaround time....

The brain of the young child is overstimulated by the new multimedia environment with its sound effects and rapidly changing, attention grabbing images. I do wonder about the effect on the attention span of the developing brain. Could the rise in case findings of Attention Deficit Hyperactivity Disorder be related to children's constant exposure to rapid-fire stimuli on their brains?...

Children's early use of the new technologies is causing a profound change in how they experience the passage of time, and they are less willing to wait for what they perceive as long periods of time....

... they are children who are unable to cope with the slightest of frustrations, and lash out aggressively. They are entitled, demanding, impatient, disrespectful of authority, often contemptuous of their peers, unempathetic, and easily "wounded."...

Their numbers are increasing. We must take note of this disturbing trend and intervene with some urgency if we are to raise children who will care about others in society.

Marilyn B. Benoit, M.D., Alliance for Childhood

And yet, current research supporting the use of computers in the classroom has been overwhelmingly optimistic. Many students find the computer a liberating approach to writing, and they often develop a more positive approach to learning. The development of a sense of purpose, understanding the connections between their work and the real world, a willingness to rework ideas and drafts, sharing with peers, using higher level thinking skills, and developing more complex problem-solving abilities are all areas of growth for the students. However, as teachers and parents, we need to remember Dr. Benoit's warning, and balance the time our students spend on different types of texts.

Technology in the Classroom

The disparities between the electronic world outside school and the traditional school curriculum contribute to the alienation that many students feel about what goes on in their classrooms. That raises a question. How can we build on their digital literacies as we reconceptualize how to teach reading and writing?

One of the great appeals of computers for students is that they are intrinsically motivating, and students have a great deal of autonomy in their investigations. For many students who have a natural predilection for solitary, fact-based activities, word processing on the computer is a natural and comfortable tool for learning. Of course, we need to move them beyond this rudimentary use of the technology to the higher order thinking — collaborating and creating opportunities that technology makes possible. We need to be aware that computer use may affect development in areas that boys should and need to cultivate, such as collaborative learning and having a meta-awareness of texts they read. We need to help students to be active and critical in their use of multimedia, and vigilant that they do not get lost in cyberspace or incorporate inaccurate or incorrect information into their written work.

How can we build on their digital literacies as we reconceptualize how to teach reading and writing?

Students today think of themselves as programmers, as interface designers when they read and generate texts on the computer. They interweave such modes as written text, sounds, animation, and video to enhance their assignments. Computers can also be used to visualize abstract concepts or to solve problems. As a result, we can no longer view the texts we use during literacy teaching as primarily written or linguistic — they are made up of images, of sounds, of movement, just as the texts that students read and enjoy at home are print and electronic. Students who are living inside the new technological literacies need to see the role of these digital movements in shaping the world they live in. Technology is part of a larger set of social relationships.

While gender differences in literacy acquisition are discussed in some detail in Chapter 4, it is important to note that girls and boys may come to technology in different ways. Although girls have narrowed the gender gaps in math and science, technology remains dominated by boys.

Girls consistently rate themselves lower than boys on computer ability, and boys exhibit higher self-confidence and a more positive attitude about computers than girls do. Boys use computers outside of school more often than girls. Just as boys prefer resources (books, magazines, websites) that favour facts over fiction, they respond to the Web, which contains an endless frontier of facts on all manner of topics, and many boys respond to the factual and multimodal (written, image, sound, animation) nature of the Internet.

Technology provides an ideal vehicle for boys to become more acquainted with literacy and being literate. In the online world, they can safely play around with technology without worrying about their image. For both boys and girls, computer skills should pivot more on building and designing than on being passive in relation to technology. We need to create new spaces for thinking of literacy in terms of the multimodal nature of texts that students read, use, and produce.

> *"…the emergence of new media opens up students' communicational landscape with new, burgeoning modes of communication."*

Jennifer Rowsell, an authority on The New Literacies, speaking at a literacy conference, noted that "the emergence of new media opens up students' communicational landscape with new, burgeoning modes of communication. We have witnessed our students' steady mastery of such standard practices as clicking, cutting and pasting, creating and updating Web pages, and even writing text codes. These practices are so tacit to their lives that they hardly give them a second thought. Practices such as these have been psychologized by our students and have become fundamental to the reading and writing process."

In his column headlined "I think, therefore I text message," San Grewal says not to worry about the high-tech newest generation — they're different, but they're fine. His exemplar is the 16-year-old son of a neighbour — referred to as Haddad.

> Haddad is part of the first generation raised in the communication age….
>
> He spends about four to five hours a day text messaging friends, surfing the Web, chatting on MSN Messenger (often while simultaneously talking on his cellphone), and says he logs even more hours on weekends….
>
> Those who worry about a younger generation that has locked itself into its metaphorical room, surrounded by laptops, scanners, cellphones and pagers, don't need to worry. Young people no longer have to venture into the outside world to be exposed to it. The new type of "user" is being shaped by today's communications….
>
> The minds of this emerging generation are collectively plugged into each other. They see the world horizontally, able to scan a wider horizon, not just what appears vertically on their monitors, but linking laterally from site to site for tidbits of connected information or

trivial knowledge.

One thing is certain — the willingness to passively stand back and let others shape your world for you is no longer the most obvious option....

Current communication has become increasingly participatory and even though some may fear that too much of this participation by young communication addicts is far too private, the reality is that it's more public than it has ever been....

As Marshall McLuhan said, "The user is the content." And today's user is involved in a reciprocal relationship. They're no longer willing to just sit idly by and be programmed.

San Grewal, *Toronto Star*, 22 June 2004

We have used technology to learn *from*: we need to know how to use technology to learn *with*.

School systems provided training for teachers in how to use the technology and how to use the technology with students so that they could learn from the technology. Computers were, in the most part, introduced to teachers as the latest in a long line of alternate presentation modes for transmitting information. Hence, a formalized and formidable focus on software for instructional purposes followed. Some of the software has proven to help students learn specific concepts and skills.

> *...improved learning can be linked with technology.*

The real potential of technology, however, does not lie in the learning *from*; the power is in learning *with* — using the technology as a tool for understanding concepts and thinking about ideas in new ways. As learning results from thinking, thinking about ideas is preferable to pre-fashioned activities based on ideas. Ensuring students learn *with* not only *from* technologies to design, create and invent will require professional development and support for teachers and school leaders. School districts need to be strategic and systematic in creating conditions and providing the means for technology to be used to continuously improve acquisition of literacy skills.

Communication technologies used as tools for learning assist students in doing research, seeking and analyzing information, creating new insights and ideas and applying what they learn. Technology can foster success for all learners. This desired outcome depends upon learning through knowledge construction in real-life situations. Students want more relevant, authentic learning experiences, and real-life situations are infinitely more possible, on an ongoing basis, in a rich technology-supported learning environment where students read, write and discuss as they problem solve using wide-ranging texts, real data sets, simulations, and visual representations.

Recent research has clearly demonstrated that improved learning can be linked with technology. Students develop reading, writing and discussing skills and mathematical concepts better when their learning includes technology. Technology engages learners and they spend more time on task.

New technologies and tools, while their potential for creating enriching teaching and learning is very exciting, do have limitations depending on the approach that is taken in implementing their use in the daily life of the classroom. If the focus for researchers and educators is mainly the flexibility of the tools for various settings and the access it affords learners, rather than the impact/success of the tools in the literacy learning process for individual learners, the real power of the technology won't be felt. Energy and resources will be invested without the promising pedagogical benefits that we know can come when students use the technology to collaborate to construct meaning and expand their communicative competencies.

> *Technology engages learners and they spend more time on task.*

It seems that rarely a day goes by without some new development in technology, whether it's converging multimedia, new ways to communicate and explore ideas, or the availability of goods and services — including learning programs and digital content — anywhere, anytime.... The explosion of new technologies and multimedia is expected to continue. Technology will be pervasive and a "given" in most children's lives, in their homes, their entertainment and their communication with friends and family. They will come to school with expectations that the same kinds of technology and multimedia will be pervasive in their schools. Most if not all jobs will require young people to have a range of skills in using technology and to continue learning new technology skills in the workplace.... [L]ifelong learners will use technology to develop skills and relationships, to gain, construct and share knowledge, to think critically, solve problems and make decisions. The definition of literacy in the future is likely to include not just the ability to read and write, but also basic technological, visual and information literacy. With the rapid expansion of knowledge, students will need to be able to find, sort, assess, make decisions and apply knowledge and information to a variety of problems and situations.

Every Child Learns: Every Child Succeeds
Report of the Alberta Commission on Learning, 2003

When the focus is on using technology to learn rather than concentrating on learning about technology per se, there are clear and connected language outcomes for students:

- Technology can help students be more productive and creative by providing access to engaging ways of representing ideas both verbally and graphically.
- Technology can help students collaborate to publish, interact with, and use a wide range of media and formats to communicate information and ideas.
- Technology can help students to research more effectively by using tools to locate, evaluate and collect information. Technology also facilitates the processing, reporting and presenting of conclusions and insights from data.
- Technology can help students work with others, including peers and telementors (online advisors), to solve problems and make informed decisions.

We are also aware of potential drawbacks in using the Internet. Information on the Web is frequently inaccurate and at times incorrect.
- The adage "buyer beware" can be borrowed here to become "reader beware." Anyone can post a website on the Internet, and, as a result, information is not checked for accuracy. Encourage students to use websites from established institutions and businesses.
- We need to monitor students as they use the Internet to ensure that they are where they should be.
- Not all search engines are created equal. As well, some students will be able to manoeuvre in any environment, while others will search in vain for hours. Proficient peers can act as tutors to classmates who have less experience finding information on the Internet.

- We need to limit students' time on the Internet given the demand for use by other students. Wandering the Internet, while entertaining, can be extremely time-consuming.

Schools must join the technology-rich world of today's learners. Students, particularly those who are not meek and not neat, respond to technology-enhanced learning opportunities and will demonstrate their ability as they have not previously — thereby, teacher expectations can be raised for those learners.

Learning with technology provides students a mix of fun and learning in ways that cannot be matched by traditional classrooms which are based on the teacher as expert and the student as receiver of mediated information. The ideal classroom is one where technology is used as a tool to understand concepts and to think, where the information available through technology is controlled by the learner, available when the learner is ready, and embedded in networks of mutual interests among peers.

There is no doubt that technology can enhance instructional practice. Teachers can dramatically change their practice and students can have far superior learning opportunities with new strategies for learning through such tools as Knowledge Forum — a learning tool in which students read, write and discuss in order to pose and develop hypotheses and essential questions. Building collaborative competencies among students and among their teachers as they reflect on practice together is greatly supported by technology.

Using technology to learn

Many very able students suffer from learning disabilities which can impede their progress in reading and writing. Students with outstanding conceptual and analytical capacity can sometimes be challenged by difficulties in writing both in terms of legibility and spelling and syntax. The use of the computer to assist such students with their writing has a large impact on the students' motivation and progress. Wherever possible, students with special needs should be encouraged to use technology to assist with the writing process and to allow for collaboration and exploration of existing and new ideas. The computer can be a great homogenizer in the classroom and remove the stigma and embarrassment which students with writing difficulties experience when shaping their written work.

Name of student: Paul
Grade or Age: Grade 4

Paul is in a grade 4 gifted class. On my first day of a volunteer placement in this class, I was told by the teacher that Paul had unique circumstances. The son of two lawyers, Paul had difficulties writing and had been identified as Gifted Learning Disabled. I was later told by Paul's mother that his father and grandfather had similar difficulties.

I noticed that Paul made brilliant contributions to class discussions. His ideas were insightful and well thought out. He was articulate, had a wealth of knowledge, and was eager to learn. He was interested in reading non-fiction and was particularly fascinated by science. Although a strong, fluent reader, in comparison to his gifted classmates, Paul's reading was somewhat less developed, appearing slower and more laboured at times.

In spite of his expressive nature, Paul had great difficulty transferring his ideas onto paper and his writing was for the most part incoherent and illegible as his spelling was barely decodable. He reversed most of his letters and would begin writing from the opposite side of the page. Orally, Paul did not have any trouble spelling words or relating his ideas in a clear fashion. However, in writing, he was not able to convey his ideas.

To accommodate his needs, Paul's mother and teacher encouraged him to use the computer for word processing. With the support of the computer, Paul did not have to struggle with writing conventions. At the computer, it was not apparent that this child had any difficulty with writing. At home, almost all of Paul's writing was done on his home computer, but Paul had many reservations about writing on the computer in class.

In my opinion, Paul's comfort level in writing at home could quite possibly stem from the fact that writing difficulties ran in Paul's family and he likely felt that home was a risk-free environment. Knowing that his father understood what he was experiencing, it is conceivable that Paul found solace writing in the comfort of his home.

This experience has exposed me to the benefits of computer technology in literacy development. Paul was fortunate to have resources available at home and at school to accommodate his needs. Had these supports not been in place, Paul would have probably slipped through the cracks of our education system. For me, Paul's story has revealed the complexities surrounding the diverse needs of students within literacy development and the myriad of factors that affect student learning at all levels.

Exploring and valuing all of a student's strengths

Families that are inclined to literacy activities such as reading, writing and discussion of traditional print materials may fail to support other literacy skills such as television and film literacy and the literacies required to play video games successfully. When these activities are discouraged, opportunities to develop general literacy are lost. There are many pathways to understanding and the multiple intelligences of our students create many openings for learning.

Name of Student: Daniel
Age or Grade: Grade 7
By: Larry Swartz

Daniel is a twelve-year-old boy who lives in Toronto. He is a sixth grade student at a small private school. Daniel's literacy strengths and weaknesses raise interesting questions, and since he is a friend of the family, I chose this young reader in order to add background to this literacy profile. Daniel's reading and writing experiences represent a child with support and encouragement from both home and school, but he has not made as much progress as others his age. I felt that by examining his different literacies, along with issues in regard to his schooling, we perhaps can remember how difficulties with print literacy affect a student's day-to-day life activities, and how we need to build support at home and in school for students who are labelled with learning disabilities.

Daniel is surrounded by a family who very much encourages 'printed' literacy. His home is filled with books, magazines, and newspapers. His father and mother are both teachers, and his sisters are excellent readers. Daniel would often hear his family talking about authors, newspaper columns, best-sellers, and literary gossip. As a young child, Daniel was read to each night, and the bookshelves in his room are filled with books that include children's classics and contemporary titles such as the *Harry Potter* series.

Daniel, however, has never been particularly interested in books. As a youngster, he seemed to prefer watching movies to being read to by his parents. It is interesting, too, that Daniel did not seem involved with art or making crafts, despite the fact that his parents set up an art table in the kitchen filled with crayons, paints and paper. He did, however, enjoy hands-on activities and would often play with his action figures.

In the second grade, Daniel seemed to have some difficulty processing written words and images, and was diagnosed as having a learning disability. Reading and writing do not come easily to him, and his spelling skills are weak. It is obvious that little pleasure is gained from either reading or writing. Getting homework done each night has been a struggle, although he does get constant support from his mother and father, who have always kept involved with Daniel's schooling. A tutor was hired to provide Daniel with some extra literacy support.

Daniel has a number of other literacies that he explores and enjoys. He enthusiastically watches television and enjoys comedy shows, especially animated shows.

He is fond of playing video games and willingly spends a lot of time on the computer and with various game systems. He is able to discuss episodes of favourite shows he has watched, and comments on what he thought was funny or surprising. Daniel's household has three television sets, and he owns a computer and a number of video games. His parents try to limit the amount of time he spends on these two pastimes, but Daniel still perseveres.

At school, Daniel chooses to participate in a number of extracurricular activities and it is these events which give Daniel a sense of worth and pride. He excels in many athletic areas, and is a champion hockey player. Besides sports, Daniel has taken an interest in drama and has recently performed in two school plays. He seems to really enjoy theatre and has shown himself to be a talented young actor. Learning lines has not been a problem for him, despite his literacy challenges. In fact, he has tutored some of his friends who were having difficulty learning lines. When Daniel reads scripts, he does so fluently, and does so in spite of his learning disability.

Daniel enjoys comic books, and purchases collections of comic strips such as *Garfield* and *Calvin and Hobbes*. He is also keen to read material connected to his extracurricular activities, such as the programs from the theatre and the newsletters from his sports team. He seldom chooses to read novels, other than those determined by his teacher. Daniel is a sensitive and patient young man. He communicates well, and friends and family find him to be energetic and caring.

Daniel's support system is strong. He attends a committed school, yet academics are challenging for him. This seems to be a particular problem for Daniel, not only because his family values printed texts, but because "book" literacy is the mainstay of his school. The strengths Daniel has in other literacies, such as television and computers, aren't as useful academically. His new interest in theatre may serve him well, though, since it provides an alternative to his curriculum studies as well as a connection to school.

In order to enhance his literacy skills, Daniel could more effectively incorporate the use of his computer in his literacy struggles: specific programs could be employed to assist him with completing his projects and his homework effectively. Revisiting the concept of a trusted tutor would also provide an avenue of needed support for this boy. Daniel is growing in his strategies for handling printed texts, but requires continued support and guidance at home and in school to become an independent reader and writer.

Liz Spittal-Coté
Program Teacher

Calgary Board of Education, Alberta Initiative
for School Improvement (AISI)
Works in 22 schools in Calgary

"You have to get used to being 'resource-less' at the start. You bring in resources in response to your learners, You can't know what you're going to do until you know your learners."

Literacy strategies that work

- foster the development of "essential questions" which learners can pursue in their reading and writing and discussions;
- focus on inquiry-based instruction leading to strategic learning and teaching in response to students' questions, intentions and interests;
- use students' questions to direct classroom activity in order to support learners who are struggling with reading and writing;
- find authentic materials, texts, print and media resources to fit students' questions, not the other way around;
- use multimedia approaches to enhance students' capacity to read, write, discuss and represent their understandings;
- support metacognition by having students use a "split-page technique" of note taking where students note their insights about their own learning;
- use websites such as Tom Cobb's Compleat Lexical Tutor to colour code academic or difficult words which may be challenging to students;
- recycle difficult words in a variety of contexts;
- use key visuals and graphics to illustrate meaning of words and ideas;

- use "anticipation guides" to introduce and/or explain topics to help students consider ideas before they read the text and then come back to them after the reading;
- "ratchet" (a term developed by Carol Ann Tomlinson, Virginia) the levels of complexity of reading, writing and speaking tasks. For example, when learning about conflict resolution through the United Nations:

  (i) start with first-hand experience such as negotiating and accommodating barriers with classmates over a given issue;

  (ii) move to second-hand exposure where the students observe or read about others in a conflict resolution situation and relate it to a personal experience;

  (iii) finally, move into abstraction to consider the conflict resolutions used at the UN.

Other points to consider:

- check on texts' readability to use appropriate software;
- combine differentiated instructional strategies for diverse learners with inclusionary, pro-social practices to encourage cooperation and empathy in the classroom.

CHAPTER 3

Joining the Literacy Club: How Reading Works

The Process of Reading

Most of us in education can remember the "Eureka" moment when we first realized we could read. However, if we are to help our students become better readers, we must understand the reading process. We want them to think about what they are reading, make their own discoveries, and share their understandings with others to extend the meanings they are making. Literary understanding grows as students begin to grasp the many reasons why authors write and the many choices made in the writing, not only of topic and storyline, but also of style and technique. Their world views expand as they relate an author's concerns to their own lives. The reading process is all of this — "understanding" words on a page is only a small part of it.

Novice readers need extensive opportunities to work with a variety of materials for a variety of purposes, both in school and at home...

Novice readers need extensive opportunities to work with a variety of materials for a variety of purposes, both in school and at home — stories, poems, non-fiction selections, manuals, newspapers, magazines, computers and cartoons. We want them to see reading as a satisfying, purposeful endeavour that brings pleasure, knowledge, and discovery. They need time both to read and respond, privately or publicly, free from ridicule or a sense of failure. If reading is to become a lifelong habit, students' interactions with texts must result in satisfaction. Our aim is to make students' experiences with print so positive that they will continue to read without us.

Generally, youngsters follow what can be considered a continuum of reading development. However, they do not always master specific strategies in a strategic order. That is, they may have difficulty with one technique, and yet will have gained a strategy typically used by a more fluent reader. For example, a young reader in the primary grades might read "stegosaurus" before "and" or "the." As well, literacy competencies may vary according to the text being read, or the situation in which students find themselves reading. In a pressured reading lesson, or an oral reading assessment with the teacher, a text can often be a literacy failure because of the nature of the learning experience.

When teachers assess their students' reading ability, the majority of the behaviours fall on a particular place in the continuum. Then, teachers watch to note if students make gains that will move them into the next stage of reading.

Since reading is an individual process, one of the best indicators a teacher can use to assess growth is the student's development over the year. In order to do this, it is necessary to establish a baseline of each student's skills and knowledge in a portfolio — a collection of information that reveals and illustrates the student's literacy development. In this way, as teachers assess students through the year, they can return to the baseline to see where each student has made gains. If teachers can identify the various stages of growth for an individual student, they can have a much clearer picture of a student's difficulties, and what is required for the student to become an effective and successful reader.

> *Sadly, some adults remain excluded from the literacy club.*

Learning to read, and then continuing to grow as a reader, can be a complicated journey for some youngsters, and sadly, some adults remain excluded from the literacy club. A colleague told us a poignant story from her childhood, when she lived on a farm on the prairies. Each Friday evening after dinner, her father and the hired hand would move into the front parlour and shut the sliding door to the dining room. Because the hired hand was illiterate, the father would read aloud the letter that the hired hand had received from his betrothed living in their homeland. The family sat around the table, offering privacy to the two men in the next room, all the while listening to the sobs of the hired hand, alone and distanced from his loved one.

Depending upon the text, some find themselves unable to make sense of the print — lacking background with the content (a science discovery), afraid of the format (a legal document), unable to read the words (a medical report), too nervous to make meaning (a public speech), unfamiliar with the medium (a computer chat room), or new to the language (ESL). There are still thousands of non-readers who are unable to interpret the simplest printed text, but with our help as literacy mentors, with appropriate teaching, they will be able to join the literacy club.

The Early Reader

Early readers enter kindergarten with some of the skills and concepts they need to become readers already in place. These children generally enjoy meeting texts in school, since most of their literacy experiences have involved being read to by family members or caregivers. Books, then, represent pleasure and entertainment for them. Many children will have favourite stories they like to hear again and again. These readers have developed a sense of story, and enter into the experience readily.

Early readers will often pick up a book and approximate reading by holding it the right way, stopping the reading while they turn the page and finishing the story exactly on the last page. They are learning that texts give cues to reading, that print on a page matches certain words, that pictures support the story, that books are read from front to back, that text flows from left to right and that reading is an authentic activity. When children "read" books in this way, they are preparing themselves to become readers.

> *When children "read" books in this way, they are preparing themselves to become readers.*

Early readers know that print carries meaning and they are aware of sources of print around them — in books, on products, on labels, on signs, and so on. While they recognize many of these words in context, they may not carry over this knowledge when they see the words in isolation. These readers may not know how sounds are represented by letters. Phonemic awareness — how sounds combine to make words — and phonics — how words are written on a page — will develop during this period.

Phonemic and phonics instruction, if it is to be effective, should occur through real reading activities, such as using rhymes, songs, books with strong patterns, and word games. These activities focus children's attention on sounds and the corresponding letter or letters that represent them. It is only when children have a knowledge of sound-letter correspondence that they can begin to read and write independently and transfer knowledge from one situation to another.

The Emergent Reader

Emergent readers, like early readers, enjoy listening to stories and have favourite books that they seemingly never tire of. Children at this stage know that books can provide them with entertainment and information and they see themselves as capable of reading them.

These youngsters have refined their knowledge of how books work, and realize that the purpose of print is to record or share meaning, and that it is fixed. They are beginning to rely on semantic and syntactic cueing systems to predict events, and can retell sequences of events. These children are interested in developing their print abilities. They like to have their stories transcribed, which they can then read back to a teacher or parent.

To help emergent readers develop knowledge of how writing reflects spoken words, it is necessary to create environments where children are surrounded by print. Teachers or parents need to show examples of how print is used and give children plenty of opportunities to read books successfully, particularly pattern books and books with detailed illustrations. Shared reading, of course, brings these books alive and directs children to focus on functions of print. Finally, publishing children's own stories gives them real reasons to write and reinforces the major purposes of writing — to record and to share.

> *To help developing readers in their literacy development, they need to consolidate a strong sense of story.*

The Developing Reader

Developing readers can read some texts independently and successfully. Children at this stage of reading often enjoy books by a favourite author, including books in a series, and it is during this period that they come to recognize characteristics of various genres. Using this knowledge, and their experience in reading, children begin to develop personal literary interests.

At this stage, their knowledge of sound-letter correspondence is growing, and they can recognize and write letter groups such as blends and digraphs. Their knowledge of sight words is also growing, and they can read these words in both familiar and unfamiliar contexts.

Readers blend four cueing systems — pragmatic, semantic, syntactic, and phonographemic (phonics) — to help them make meaning. They are able to self-monitor their reading, identifying and correcting miscues, and can substitute words that make sense when they are unsure of a text. At this level, children are reading silently. Some children may still finger point or say the words softly to themselves. As their reading ability develops further, they will discontinue these practices.

To help developing readers in their literacy development, we need to help them consolidate a strong sense of story. Teachers can build upon developing readers' enjoyment of independent reading, particularly with familiar texts, as well as their interest in discussing stories in small groups, and the value they place on connections between reading and writing. As part of their literacy program, teachers should introduce chapter books and simple novels and ask students to retell the plots of stories they have read. To imbue a meta-awareness of texts, children at this stage need to be encouraged to recognize characteristics of genres of texts. As well, they need to increase knowledge of literary elements and the materiality of texts (for example, the cover, illustrations and so on). Developing readers should also recognize phonics generalizations and have a growing vocabulary of sight words.

The Fluent Reader

Fluent readers have arrived at a point where they have built up an extensive sight vocabulary and thus are free from the time-consuming word analysis that may have occurred at previous stages. These readers can read a range of texts for a variety of purposes, read silently, link new information with existing knowledge and adjust their style of reading to reflect the type of text being read.

> *Just as they are becoming independent in their reading, so, too, are they becoming independent in their writing.*

This is a critical stage in reading. Some students may begin to lose their enthusiasm for reading because books may appear too challenging or they no longer find themselves as captivated by story. In these cases, we must select books that students enjoy and that they can read successfully, all the while avoiding habits and classroom routines that limit student choice. Students need to continue to confirm reading as an act that entertains them, that brings them satisfaction, that adds to their knowledge and that is undertaken for genuine reasons.

Just as they are becoming independent in their reading, so, too, are they becoming independent in their writing. These students are learning to write in a variety of forms for a variety of audiences and purposes. In addition, they are improving the quality of their written work through editing and proofreading and are mastering the conventions of the language.

The Independent Reader

These independent readers read texts independently and silently. The style of reading they choose reflects the material being read and these readers monitor their reading for understanding. These students can read a range of books, as well as novels, that reflect other cultures, other times and other ways of looking at the world. They are capable of interpreting complex plots and characterization, and need to be challenged to move ahead on their own, using fiction, non-fiction and computers.

To further the development of independent readers, it is important to encourage them to read a range of texts in a variety of ways, through such means as independent reading, shared reading and literature circles. Since their writing often reflects their reading knowledge, they can be encouraged to respond to texts they have read in innovative ways.

The Primary Years

The ways in which children encounter print in the first years of school may determine their view of reading and writing for the rest of their lives. Classroom experiences with printed words should be a natural part of the play and learning that arise from the need to communicate. Children who talk, model, paint, paste, and draw are already using symbols to represent thought. They will see words and letters as just another code that lets them explore and communicate. Our job at this time is to convince children that print is meaningful, that print embodies thought, and that written language can help them make sense of their experiences.

> *The literacy-based classroom is full of print — signs, books, magazines, and stories.*

As the children focus on the reading and writing processes, we work to expand and extend their language development, to help them make sense of what they are reading and of what they are writing. They need to assess their writing through their own reading to discover how what they want to say can be fully realized by the reader. We can build on the knowledge of literary patterns the children already possess and let the children take charge of the meaning-making in ways they understand, as they build narratives, add dialogue, and discuss the essentials of a story.

The literacy-based classroom is full of print — signs, books, magazines, computer screens and stories. When they see their names around the room, on their belongings, on charts, and on bulletin boards, children become aware of written messages — how they help us communicate, give us information, direct us. They notice the teacher using print — on memos, lists, and charts; it becomes an active force in their lives, as they dictate their stories to others or write them with their own invented spelling. They experiment with the forms they need for various functions of writing — labels, lists, stories, captions, letters, and journals. As the teacher reads aloud to them, the children experience the power of print and the joy of story. They grow into seeing themselves as readers as they join in the shared reading of texts they can follow. They listen to older children read aloud, choose what they want to read at some times, and read assigned texts with a group at others. They grow into seeing themselves as writers as they keep private journals, engage in group record keeping, and reflect in print on their own pleasures and concerns so that others may read their thoughts. They learn to revise their writing so that other readers can understand what they want to convey, moving toward the use of conventional spelling and punctuation and control over form.

It is in the primary years that children become aware that they can rely on print to carry a message. They discover that a book is used in a particular order — from front to back; a page is read from left to right and top to bottom; the message is revealed line by line, word by word, and letter by letter, the style of print and the punctuation giving clues to intonation; pictures can be used to predict or demonstrate what the print has to say; word-attack strategies and spelling skills can help in making meaning from text. As they become familiar with various functions of print, they will find that effective readers are always making predictions and connections. They see how stories, poems, lists, and instructions "work" as they absorb the flow of language and the internal patterns and structures. In each classroom, there will be students working at different stages of literacy growth. Many emergent readers make rapid progress through programs that "scaffold" their experiences with print, and developing readers move into independent modes with texts. However, some youngsters will require intervention programs to move them into literacy success.

> *...some youngsters will require intervention programs to move them into literacy success.*

The Middle Years

The years between eight and thirteen are the "quantity" years, when students gain reading power through in-depth experiences with biographies, with science books, on screen, and, especially, with novels. Students often enjoy reading several books by a favourite author or a series of books about a familiar set of characters. Common themes link the most widely read books — humour, school, friends, mystery, fantasy. Yet readers' tastes may shift and develop almost from day to day. Boys and girls may prefer different types of books, and peer group pressures may influence their reading choices. While students should be given as many opportunities as possible for choice in their independent reading, we can still bring fine stories to their attention that will interest them, satisfy their needs, and present a wider view of the world, free of stereotypes and sexist portrayals.

The range of reading levels in the middle years varies widely. Those students who have developed into mature, independent readers need to deepen their reading experiences by moving into quality texts alongside their quantity reading. There are many young adult novels at an appropriate intellectual and emotional level that will present these young readers with problems and situations of greater complexity, subtle characterization, and multifaceted plot structures than many of today's paperback bestsellers. Stories from other countries, other cultures, or other contexts can challenge their concepts and ideas. We must also remember that even the many readers who have reached a level of independence have listening abilities that still outreach their reading abilities; it is still important to read to them.

Adolescent Readers

> *It is still important to read to them.*

As young readers move into adolescence, their lives, both in and out of school, take on new complexities and responsibilities. Often, time for independent reading disappears amid the swirl of activities. Many schools, such as the one in the following report, attempt to schedule time for reading within the school day to support literacy growth, especially for those students who are not achieving in formal assessment measures.

"Reading Slump Affects Tests" explores the possible reasons teenagers can't pass literacy tests.

"Between sports, high-school homework, part-time jobs and the opposite sex, the early teen years serve up so many distractions. Kids can fall into a reading slump they may never come out of," warned spokesperson Alexandra Dunsmuir of the literacy advocacy group ABC Canada.

Turning 13 can convert even the most passionate pre-teen bookworm, warned Sandra Huehn of literacy group Frontier College.

"But with reading, you either use it or lose it," said Huehn, who runs free homework clubs for inner-city children.

At Toronto's Jarvis Collegiate, where literacy scores stayed about the same this year, principal Pauline McKenzie has kids "use it" every day, in an unusual 25-minute mandatory "reading period" every afternoon.

"Everyone in the school stops and reads for pleasure, including the teachers, the secretaries, myself and even the caretakers if they possibly can get free," said McKenzie.

Louise Brown, Education Reporter
Toronto Star, 1 May 2003

As this report suggests, reading requires support from the entire school community, both in establishing a literacy environment and in offering strategies for growth. Of course, students will be in different stages of development while placed in one classroom: some are avid voluntary readers while others are still struggling; some write easily with good command of transcription skills while others lack confidence to put pencil to paper; some speak up in book discussions, eager to share their responses, while others draw back and remain silent. As they attempt to find their own voices, they discover the complexities of relationships and the tentative nature of their roles in the school community.

Adolescent readers are expected to read and write independently and, more often, to read longer and more difficult texts in a variety of curriculum areas, to read faster and more selectively, to write coherently with their own voices, to remember more information and to make integrated connections with the curriculum. There are new words and terms to learn in all of the different subject areas; some of the texts may be outdated, inaccessible or poorly written; readers of widely differing abilities are expected to read the same resources with few support structures. If we collaborate with them in negotiating how we will explore the curriculum as language learners, we can observe from the inside out how each student learns best, and select our strategies carefully, so that young people do not spend their time attending to what they already know, or as Cris Tovani says in her book *I Read It But I Don't Get It*, pretending to be learning when they are completely lost. When students feel the liberation that comes from having a say in what they read and write, they have a stake in creating and maintaining a classroom that stimulates and supports deep learning, freeing the teacher to concentrate on how best to guide, inform and strengthen students' abilities.

If we collaborate with them in negotiating how we will explore the curriculum as language learners, we can observe from the inside out how each student learns best...

We need to make the solitary acts of reading and writing socially constructed events if we want to promote literacy development in young people. Jeff Wilhelm asserts in *You Gotta Be the Book* that the "peer group imperative" demonstrated every day by our students may be our greatest classroom asset. There is such satisfaction in watching developing readers enter a discussion with a group about a shared selection, as they begin to notice how they create meaning, to wrestle with ideas, to prove a point by reading a portion of the text, to ask questions about the comments of group members, to draw inferences from the discussion and the words on the page, and to gain insights from their own experiences with print. They are constructing meaning together, making sense of their own responses to what they have read and heard, mediated by the ideas and feelings of the group members. Suddenly, reading has become an interactive process, a socially constructed learning experience. These students are involved in exploring and interpreting texts as authentic readers, supported and encouraged by effective classroom practice.

Cueing Systems for Reading

Reading is an interactive process in which the reader uses a variety of strategies for comprehension. Readers of all ages use the same overall strategies in making meaning from print. First, they prepare, often intuitively, as they consider the author, the type of material, or the topic. During the act of reading, they sample the text, confirming or rejecting possible meanings, looking for answers, and forming new questions. They apply the necessary strategies — reading along, pausing to consider meanings accrued so far, hypothesizing, re-reading, omitting words until they have more information, reading ahead to build additional context to modify or clarify meaning, or simply stopping because the material is unsuitable or too difficult. They respond to both the intent and content of the print, developing a personal interpretation that reflects their own linguistic resources and world experience.

> *Readers read to comprehend.*

Readers read to comprehend. While reading a text, they subconsciously ask if it makes sense. When they attempt to read printed resources, they draw on many different kinds of knowledge to make meaning; they go back and forth, hypothesizing about and confirming ideas using cues found in the print — the semantic context, the syntactic structures, and the visible features of the words and letters. Everything matters when reading; the reader must bring all kinds of information together in order to grasp the sense of the text. Effective readers balance and integrate the various cues into the broadest possible construct for comprehension.

Pragmatic Cues (Knowing about Books)

Written material is organized in practical ways, ways that work. Chinese and Hebrew are laid out differently on the page and in the book from English. Shopping lists are different from statistical tables, just as instructions are different from novels. As teachers, we must help readers understand these pragmatic contexts within which all the other cueing systems function.

Semantic Cues (Knowing about the World)

Being able to read the words correctly does not necessarily result in comprehension. Readers must be able to relate these words to what they signify; they need to comment on the subject matter. Semantic cues relate the reading material to known facts, ideas, or concepts so that readers can integrate new information with what they already understand.

Syntactic Cues (Knowing about Language)

Syntactic cues allow readers to transfer their knowledge of oral language to printed material. Knowledge of common sentence patterns and the functions of words within sentences enables readers to predict upcoming words. In the sentence "The angry dog chased the frightened cat," readers can choose the type of word that follows the second "the" from a limited range of alternatives — adjectives and nouns. As they develop, readers become familiar with the language patterns used in writing rather than in speech, and are able to predict more successfully through these more sophisticated syntactic cues.

> *Being able to read the words correctly does not necessarily result in comprehension.*

Phonographemic Cues (Knowing about Print)

Phonographemic cues, often called "phonics," are the relationships between the sounds (phonemes) and written symbols (graphemes) of language. Readers use them mostly to help confirm guesses. As Frank Smith told us, "All reading teachers know implicitly that phonics is easy if you already have a good idea of what the word is in the first place. Students who can predict that the next word is likely to be either cow, horse or sheep will not need much knowledge of spelling-to-sound correspondences to decide which it is. In fact, it is through such prediction that a mastery of useful phonics is acquired." Thus, phonographemic cues are probably used in reading less often and to less purpose than many people suspect. English has no simple one-to-one correspondence between spoken and written forms; there are often many ways to represent the same sound. Readers use semantic and syntactic cues to develop generalizations about letters and sounds.

The Cueing Systems at Work

In reading, all four cueing systems are constantly at work and the effectiveness of one is increased by the use of the others. When readers have sufficient background experience with the type of reading material, prior knowledge of the subject matter, and familiarity with the language patterns, they use detailed visual information only occasionally, relying for the most part on an ability to predict accurately. This lets them read fast and fluently. When the subject matter, the vocabulary and/or sentence structure are unfamiliar, the reader is less able to predict and must look more closely at the print. The reading rate slows down and more re-readings may be necessary. Thus a letter from a friend is easier to read than an involved technical manual. Proficient readers use a minimum of cues to derive the maximum of meaning from print and are continually compromising between speed and accuracy.

In reading, all four cueing systems are constantly at work and the effectiveness of one is increased by the use of the others.

Literacy programs that incorporate all four cueing systems with students in the early and middle years can dramatically reduce the number of reading problems experienced by today's adolescents and young adults. We need to promote thoughtful interaction with what is being read through our response activities, to allow readers to be able to select relevant, significant information from the text, make sense of it, and integrate it with what they already know into their own knowledge construction.

Talk as a Way to Meaning

Interestingly, talk is probably the main tool in promoting literacy. As the students dig inside the text, they revise and remake their own interpretations in the light of what others in their group reveal about their own attempts at making meaning. In a small group, individuals can put forward their own concerns. Before reading, they can meet together to predict, anticipate, and set the stage for the narrative. During and after reading, they can use talk — invisible print that can be edited and re-formed so easily — to make both personal and collective meaning. Talk can be the starting point for story projects of all kinds — research, role-playing, writing, storytelling, reading aloud, painting. Some discussions can be tape-recorded for playback as clarification and consolidation or for another group to hear. Sharing thoughts and feelings with

True readers are always in a state of "becoming."

others who have read some of the same books can lead to quite sophisticated literary generalizations and understanding. Readers — that is, people who willingly pick up books and read because they value the experience — do not materialize overnight. It takes time to build a frame of reference for complex texts and to become confident as a reader. True readers are always in a state of "becoming."

Defining Comprehension

When readers read, are they always able to make sense of what they are seeing in print? Do they connect to what the author is saying? Are the text's words or ideas too far removed from their own experiences? How can we assist readers in making sense of what they read, so that their personal understanding and satisfaction will grow and deepen from the experience? This is what is meant by "teaching comprehension."

Reading comprehension, or textual understanding, occurs when readers are able to interpret symbols in order to make meaning. A reader internalizes the accrued meanings and relates these to previous knowledge, experiences and texts read before. Comprehension is both a cognitive and emotional process, and thus, it is difficult to assess.

In order for readers to understand a text, they must be able to relate it to other texts they have read and to life experiences, thereby adding the knowledge gained from this text to their knowledge base. The strength of these connections relates directly to a reader's level of comprehension. If students cannot connect the reading to their lives, their level of comprehension will suffer, just as it will if they cannot connect this text to others they have read.

> *All students need effective comprehension strategies to grow into independent readers and writers.*

Schools need to help students develop into independent, purposeful readers who will think carefully about what they are reading. Often, readers in trouble make little sense of what they have been decoding, or they choose to ignore meaning-making completely, and give up in frustration as they fail at word calling. All students need effective comprehension strategies to grow into independent readers and writers.

Strategies For Overall Reading Growth

There are certain strategies that teachers can use to help students become better readers, regardless of where the students might be in their reading development. These include:

- basing literacy teaching on a sound theory of how we learn to read and write;
- selecting texts that students can read successfully on their own and ones that will make them want to read other texts;
- providing scaffolding opportunities for students to read increasingly difficult texts;
- encouraging students to re-read texts on occasion for the sake of

developing fluency, and to read selected texts and parts of texts in order to develop varied responses (for example, to examine the theme, the author's style, and so on);

- ensuring that students always read to make meaning and that they look for significance in what they read;
- modelling the use of strategies for reading, and modelling the use of self-assessment strategies;
- assisting students in using techniques such as sound/letter correspondence, and words within words, to advance knowledge about how words work.

> *It is vital today to include technology as a literacy resource.*

When readers develop strategies for understanding text and for monitoring their own reading, they can become fluent, independent readers who can assume control of and responsibility for their learning. Along the way, they need secure environments in which they can experience plenty of success in their reading ventures, where they feel safe to experiment and make errors or miscues in their reading. It is through these miscues that students learn to self-correct and self-monitor their reading of a text, and it is often through their miscues that students demonstrate their contextual understandings.

There are three basic understandings that serve as the foundation for our reading programs: readers expect text to make meaning; they want to make meaning with text; and their meaning-making is influenced by their previous experience and knowledge.

All readers need our time and attention, but troubled readers in particular benefit from carefully planned, timetabled opportunities for focusing on literacy growth. We need to encourage these readers to continue their reading of real texts, while at the same time assisting them in learning to use the necessary strategies.

Reading and Writing with Computers

It is vital today to include technology as a literacy resource. The websites, the chat lines, the word processors, the DVDs, the fonts, and the spellcheckers are all aspects of making meaning with words and images. School literacies need to interconnect with home literacies in moving youngsters toward becoming independent readers and writers.

As technology advances, so must our literacy practices. As a result of technology, there are different sorts of literacy practices employed today than there were twenty years ago. Practices like word processing, web searches, scanning documents, and even pointing, clicking, cutting and pasting, are now fundamental to the writing process.

More now than ever before, students need to apply critical thinking processes to texts they read on screen. All of the strategies we incorporate into our reading of books, magazines and curriculum materials apply to the texts found on emails and websites. Students need to reflect about the source of the information, the context, the author, the intent, the style, all of those qualities that effective readers take into account with every text that they read.

When working to improve reading and writing, teachers can:

- use the Internet as an instructional resource and for online learning programs;
- develop web navigation strategies with students;
- have the students use the Internet to support research and writing;
- ensure students make full use of word-processing features when publishing pieces of writing;
- encourage students to enhance their writing through fonts, colour, spreadsheets, graphs and photos;
- have students share pieces of writing with other young writers on the Internet;
- allow time for students to foster relationships with readers and writers around the world through email;
- encourage various forms of electronic communication through email, mailing lists and newsgroups;
- incorporate CDs, videotapes and films in literacy programs so that students can access different forms of information;
- have students listen to books on tape, CD, and DVD.

> *More now than ever before, students need to apply critical thinking processes to texts they read on the screen.*

The Factors Affecting Reading Comprehension

We can classify factors that have an impact on a student's understanding of a specific text in three general categories, but of course, they can overlap with each other.

The Student:

- Is the reader interested in the content of the text? Does he or she have an appreciation of what it holds for him or her?
- Is the reader able to make connections both from his or her life and from literacy experiences with other texts?
- Is the reader familiar with the ideas that are represented in the text?
- Does the reader have an awareness of the characteristics of the genre (for example, report, novel, poem)? Does this awareness cause the reader to create meanings or to become disengaged by the format of the writing?
- Does the reader know the strategies effective readers use?
- Does the reader have an understanding of the goal of reading a particular text selection? (For example, was it a test with questions, a story linked to a wider theme, or homework?)
- Did the reader choose the text to be read? Was it assigned?
- Were there opportunities for the reader to respond to the text through discussion or writing to clarify or deepen his or her understanding of the text?
- What are the attributes, opinions and behaviours of the reader and his or her peers during reading activities? Does the reader conform, act out, or work independently?

> *Does the reader know the strategies effective readers use?*

The Teacher:

- Were there authentic purposes for reading and writing?
- How much pre-text support was offered for setting the stage for the reading of the text?
- Was a careful selection of the texts made for both the interest and abilities of individuals in the class?
- Were there opportunities for building motivation to engage the reader in the reading?
- Was there a sense of ownership of the reading experience for the student?
- Did the classroom organization support intensive and extensive reading?
- Was there regular monitoring of the readers' progress in order to support their reading growth?

- Were useful prompts offered as strategies to support the reader while building comprehension with the text?
- Did the follow-up activities include reflection, re-reading, revisiting, or extending of the text, so that life and literature connections were made?
- Was there support for independent reading (for example, help with complex sections; a tape of the book)?
- Did the teacher build a relationship with the reader? As tester, mentor, or facilitator?
- The conditions surrounding the event — was it a private reading experience, a collaborative group experience, a public shared experience, a performance, or a test? Was there a choice in how the student would participate?
- The time limits for accomplishing the reading — was there a time limit? Will the work be formally assessed? Is it a component of a larger thematic framework?
- Were literacy habits such as browsing, reviewing and text selection encouraged?
- Were there varied opportunities to experience success in the reading event and to develop confidence as readers?
- Were there demonstrations and mini-lessons given by the teacher for both the class and groups, to present and support reading strategies?

> *Were there authentic purposes for reading and writing?*

The Text (printed or electronic)

- Did the text support the reader's interests and/or needs?
- Did the qualities of the language and style of the text support the reader's abilities and interests?
- Was the genre of the text selected (for example, narrative, poem) appropriate and applicable?
- Was the complexity of ideas presented in the text appropriate for the particular reader?
- Was the reader able to interpret the inference demands of the text?
- Was the level of vocabulary (for example, unfamiliar words, jargon, idioms) appropriate and accessible to the reader?
- Did the illustrations and diagrams support the print demands of the text?

• Was the writer skilful in involving the reader and in presenting ideas in a meaningful and well-crafted text?

Readers for Life

Universal education offers no guarantee that citizens will read, or find satisfaction or pleasure in reading — become readers in the full sense of the word. But there are so many literacies:

• school literacy: tests, essays, questions;
• life literacy: newspapers, magazines, literature;
• computer literacy: email, web searches, chat lines.

There are communities (and countries) where the chasm between the literate and the illiterate has become even wider. Some schools have no libraries, newspapers or curriculum texts, while others have email, hypertext, and virtual pages. How will this affect the equality of literacy in their students? Budgets in most districts are torn by the demand for books, print resources, and electronic equipment.

Carol Lyons, a noted educator, offers us a powerful statement that reminds us of how significant our teaching can be: "The limits of my language are the limits of my life." Literate beings interpret and construct meaning; therefore, all readers are in a developmental process throughout their lives. Different texts present different needs and require different approaches and strategies. School literacy is only one component of a reader and writer's world, but it is necessary for educational success, and it offers us as teachers opportunities for supporting students in difficulty and ways and means of accessing ideas in a variety of print formats and contexts. We want our students to become better readers of the texts they choose to read, the texts they are required to read, and the texts that are part of their everyday lives. They need to be actively engaged with the texts they meet.

Literacy is the foundation of learning and formal education. Without education and knowledge, social and economic development cannot take place. Strong links have been demonstrated among education, health, nutrition, and population control, particularly when girls and women are educated. This is a problem with a solution. The answers are in front of us. All we need to do is act.

"In country after country," the United Nations says in a recent report, "educating girls yields spectacular social benefits for the current generation and those to come. An educated girl tends to marry later and have fewer children. The children she does have will be more likely to survive; they will be better nourished and better educated. She will be more productive at home and better paid in the workplace. She will be better able to protect herself against HIV/AIDS and to assume a more active role in social, economic and political decision-making throughout her life."

Ann Thomson, Executive Director, USC Canada
Toronto Star, 6 September 2003

In life, we read what we need to for our work and what we want to for our daily lives: information onscreen and on paper, instructions, documents, recipes, TV guides, newspapers; we read what we choose to: magazines, books, the Internet, games, poems, song lyrics, biographies, reviews, ads, conversations with colleagues and friends, library and bookstore suggestions, interviews on radio and TV, documents from the government, and sometimes what we find lying around our doctor's office.

In school, what do our students read? What do we require them to read? What do we read with them? To them? What could we provide for them to read as a class, in groups and independently? What could we demonstrate with them using an overhead projector, PowerPoint, or multiple copies? What genres could we include in our shared reading? Which websites could we connect to in order to promote electronic literacy? What texts are they reading on their own that they could talk about?

We need to know our students in order to understand their life situations and to recognize their particular needs and interests, the things that trouble them, and what constitutes literacy success in their lives. We can listen to and read their life stories that they write in class, and we can share our own anecdotes about our literacy lives and our families. Some teachers spend a few minutes each week with a "literacy talk" about their own lives — what they have read or are reading or intend to read (at home and at school), authors they have read about, book reviews, their Internet searches, or personal correspondence. Some even keep their own reading run log as a model for their students. By demonstrating the varied aspects of our literacy lives — what we are required to read and what we choose to read, we reveal to our students that we have full literacy lives, and that popular magazines, professional books and the Internet are included.

These students in difficulty can't be ignored — they need the best instruction, including all the advantages technology can offer, and a challenging curriculum. As teachers, we can offer instructional opportunities to promote strategic reading with unfamiliar texts. These students do indeed want literacy success. They want to learn to read. They need to learn to be literate, to learn through literacy, and to learn about literacy.

Impact of Family Issues on Learning

The child in this profile is suffering from feelings of anger and uncertainty caused by his parents' separation and his unhappiness shows in his reading and writing choices. Understanding the effect family problems can have on a child's attitudes to literacy can allow the teacher to move the child along to extended choices and can ensure the child's responses to reading and writing activities are not misconstrued as inappropriate behaviour.

Name of Student: Donald
Grade or Age: Grade 5
By: Tom McKeown

Donald is a ten-year-old boy in grade 5. He has recently undergone the splitting of his parents; at one point, his father was living in the basement of their house. His mother has recently moved them out of the house to an apartment. When Donald was in grade 4, I had extensive interaction with him in the role of a guidance teacher due to bullying that Donald was doing to one particular student in grade 4.

In the area of literacy, Donald is an interesting case. He has a hard time sitting and listening to oral reading without participating in disruptive behaviour. Often, he reads comic books of a violent nature and is always drawing cartoons with "dragon ball z" as the main theme.

In class, the students have been given the opportunity of working on writing portfolios, and given choice as to the topic that they will write on and the genre that they will use, as long as they hit a variety of genres.

One of the genres that the students were given the opportunity of producing was a graphic story. Donald has become quite fixated on this type of writing and will produce nothing else. These stories are very violent, but they are a starting point for him to develop a sense of authorship. The next step for Donald is to gain a greater voice in his writing and broaden his ability to write for different audiences. That his writing is focused on such angry subject matter may be simply an expression of pain at the situation that he has found himself in, and as he is able to express himself better and build his self-esteem, perhaps it will be reflected in his work.

In his reading choices, it is rare to find Donald selecting works other than comics that focus on the battle between good and evil. During the second term, the class was given the choice of novels for literature circles. The books from which to choose included *The Lion, The Witch and the Wardrobe, Maniac Magee, Crash, Catherine Called Birdy,* and *The Hobbit Graphic Novel.* The boys in the class that have had academic and social issues, including Donald, were very anxious to get this version of *The Hobbit.* Therefore they were put in the "Hobbit" group and they are working hard at their jobs, which is encouraging for me, and I hope that from this experience Donald will be eager to move into a literature circle for a novel such as *Crash.* During this time, as well, the class is participating in an oral reading of *The Giver,* the students each have their own copy of the book. Donald seems engaged, but he seems to enjoy the story *Weasel and Milkweed* more. Overall, the goal for Donald now is to expand what he is willing to participate in his growth of literacy acquisition.

Reading for life, not for school

Students' perceptions of their reading and writing capacities are often limited by their negative responses to what they perceive as "school" material. Connections need to be made between what students naturally are drawn to in print materials such as newspapers and magazines and the reading competencies we are encouraging and developing in the school curriculum. Creating confidence in our students as successful readers is over half the battle in defeating reluctance and anxiety about reading and writing.

Name of Student: Ronald
Grade or Age: Grade 7
By: Amy Mohr

Ronald is a self-proclaimed non-reader. Both this young man and his mother have admitted that he does not like to read and that in fact getting him to read anything is a struggle. At the beginning of the year, his mother and I had a discussion about ways to get him reading this year.

What strikes me is the perception Ronald has about his own reading. He thinks that he is not good at reading and says that he does not have any interest in reading. However, there are many forms of literacy that I see him engaging in throughout the school day on a routine basis. First, in a variety of subjects throughout the day, he has to read and interact with subject textbooks. When I am looking for volunteers to read aloud, Ronald willingly offers on a frequent basis. Additionally, in our class, we receive the *Toronto Star* every day. Students are free to read and explore the newspaper whenever they have spare time or for their DEAR (Drop Everything and Read) period. We also receive *The Daily Planet*, a weekly newspaper that is targeted at teens. I often

see Ronald reading one of the newspapers and he is genuinely interested in what the paper has to offer. I also have on hand in the classroom a stack of old *National Geographic* magazines. Students are encouraged to read these magazines if they want to during the DEAR period. Again, I find Ronald reading or skimming through the magazines. Despite the perception Ronald has of reading, there are a variety of ways that he is engaged in literacy and reading each and every day.

A surprising moment occurred with Ronald when he approached me about borrowing a novel from our classroom library. It surprised me because, up until this time, he had been very reluctant to read. I enthusiastically told him that he could indeed borrow the novel. I still have to check in with him about how he is enjoying it.

Hannah Hershman
St. George's Elementary Private School, Quebec

Consultative teacher: works with teachers of students in K-3
Specialist teacher: works with reluctant readers in grades 4-6 and advises parents

"I work to establish the presence of books in lives we share together. When students see how their teacher is excited by a book, they find responding positively to reading irresistible."

"I always focus on understanding. If you can decode information on surgery in a medical journal but you don't understand it, you can't operate! I find out where the problem with comprehension is and tackle that first."

Literacy strategies that work

- set up the classroom with an inviting and changing display of a variety of books at different levels of difficulty, designed to engage students' interest;
- set up a tape and book centre where students can listen independently to tapes of stories in order to connect oral language to the printed word;
- use a guided-reading approach where students work together in a small group on a book just above their reading level using strategies such as:
  (i) looking at the cover for meaning;
  (ii) reading titles of sections or captions under pictures;
  (iii) chunking words, sentences or paragraphs; and
  (iv) skimming the book getting general impressions.
- model choosing books by having another teacher or a parent/volunteer discuss his or her reading choices to show the personal nature of book choices;
- introduce regular non-fiction reading where students are not required to read every word;
- have students focus on graphic features in the text such as captions, illustrations etc.;
- have beginning readers choose a book; read it with a partner and/or a parent volunteer; take it home to read for homework; present it;
- have students write based on their observations through recording what they see and feel in a variety of situations; students share their experiences with other students by reading their writing aloud to a partner;
- encourage writing by having students draw a picture about some aspect of the story; talk about and then write about a particular character in his or her voice; label the different parts or details of the story;
- have students keep a record of and have conversations about favourite and interesting words, and share the meanings with other students.

Assessment:

- focus on metacognition and put students' reading problems "on the table" in order to demystify them for the students and their parents. Ask questions like:
  What is hard about this reading? What am I doing that doesn't work? What am I doing that helps me understand what I am reading? What can I do about the problem?
- keep running records of students' reading to uncover patterns of strength as well as challenges with which students are dealing;
- have more than one teacher take notes on a student's reading to facilitate a dialogue on appropriate strategies.

Other points to consider:

- encourage boys to write stories that reflect their interest in action and adventure;
- help young boys who are reluctant readers by allowing frequent movement in the classroom to accommodate high levels of energy;
- have older students become reading/writing partners;
- use parent volunteers in the classroom to discuss and encourage reading.

Professional Perspectives

CHAPTER 4

Hiding in the Shadows: The Reader in Difficulty

> The grade 12 literacy course students were going to a theatre production and tour. (These students had been unsuccessful at a secondary school exit literacy examination.)
>
> Before they arrived, one of the students asked the teacher, "When you make announcements or introduce our group, could you please refer to us as the college preparatory class?"
>
> The teacher met the request, and was received with the students' applause as she joined them on the homebound bus.
>
> The power of language and the need for being sensitive to others!
>
> Joanne Hough
> School Superintendent

The students mentioned in the anecdote above expressed their gratitude to their teacher for not labelling them as "literacy failures." And in their classroom, they are continuing to strengthen their reading skills because of her.

The principles of fostering literacy development for students with special needs are consistent with those for regularly achieving students. Research by specialists working with these students indicates that they learn best in real situations where they can explore new meanings and integrate them into what they already know. We need to find ways of matching literacy competency with the demands of the curriculum in the classroom to ensure our students' progress.

Debate over how to teach reading and writing to students with learning disabilities continues between those who teach reading and writing as a sequence of component skills, and those whose teaching is based on the actual reading of texts. The constant barrage of drill and practice focuses on students' deficits, or weaknesses, and this deficit model with its ever-present reminder to students of their inadequacies has had a devastating effect on the lives of many students in remedial programs. Drill and practice can also encourage passivity in learners. The teacher decides what is to be learned and how it is to be learned. It is our view that reading and writing cannot be learned by breaking written language down into fragmented parts. We are firmly committed to integrated approaches because they are consistent with our view of the world and of learning.

Benjamin Polis is an Australian author who was diagnosed with ADHD (attention deficit/hyperactivity disorder) in 1989. He believed there should be a book about a young person being impulsive, written from the point of view of an insider. The result was *Only a Mother Could Love Him,* published when Benjamin was nineteen years old.

In *Only a Mother Could Love Him,* Benjamin Polis compares the obstacles of a school day for ADHD kids to the building of a volcano. By 3 PM, four or more layers have been poured:

"You pick up your son and he seems really happy. You believe he is happy because he had a good day at school. But really he is so happy because he is out of the school and in the sanctuary of people who love him and don't treat him differently. Your son goes home and throws his bag on the floor.... It's now time to do homework. But you know and he knows that it's not going to happen without a fight. You turn the television off and you have successfully triggered off the volcano of anger. But you are thinking, 'What the hell did I do that was so bad?' ... Your son then goes into a rage of anger, yelling and swearing at you. But you're not at fault, you're just the lava field where your son can release the anger built up over the day....

Why is it the parent who receives the raw end of the violence? It's not that your son hates you and doesn't love you. It's the exact opposite. He does love you and that's why he does it.... He knows that if he explodes like this you will be there tomorrow and still love him. You are your child's lava field and like lava fields they are used over and over again to release the pressure."

USA Today
9 June 2003

The number of students identified as having ADD with a neuro-developmental problem seems to have increased over the last several years. Some researchers suggest that many students show similar patterns of behaviour because social and environmental changes have disturbed their capacity to regulate themselves. A large number of boys today are labelled ADD, but not diagnosed as such by specialists. Although no one denies the difficulties and disruptions that these students cause, they might become proficient readers and writers with more effective literacy programs and resources. We will need to build support for our efforts in a crowded classroom.

> *Students in difficulty need to experience what successful literacy events feel like...*

We want these students to experience what successful literacy events feel like in their classrooms, so they will feel cared about and supported in their struggle toward independence as readers and writers. We will need to enlist their participation as they "revalue" their literacy selves, and as we cooperatively develop a comprehensive and inclusive program for reading and writing. They will need to make choices in their literacy lives, to sense ownership of their own reading and writing by selecting some of the books and resources they read, the topics they write about, and the projects they research. They will care more about activities they feel they own — those in which they will want to invest their time and interest.

Students in difficulty need to experience what successful literacy events feel like, to know that there is hope for recovery, that they will be supported in their struggle to grow toward independence; they need to become real readers and writers. Very few students are unable to master literacy. Therefore, we will need to assess and help many different types of struggling readers and writers, to find out what they can do and build on their competencies so that they can move forward and recognize that they are indeed improving. We design and implement assessment strategies that lead us to understand their specific needs as struggling readers; our practice grows from our assessments, so that these students can one day succeed in formal evaluation tasks.

Effective Teaching for Literacy

At the very least, literacy means being able to read and write what you need to, and then what you want to. For many students in our schools, reading and writing are difficult events to be dismissed or ignored. They find little satisfaction in reading books for pleasure, and writing is always unpopular. In assisting dependent or troubled readers, then, we need to establish specific purposes for each literacy event, since each may have different requirements.

1. Curriculum textbooks and course work present their own difficulties for students to handle. If the material to be covered is complex, unfamiliar or uninteresting, we will need to build background before reading, guide them through the text with careful teaching, or present a mini-lesson on how this particular format of text works. These literacy strategies apply to screen text as well. Because it is found on a computer does not make a text necessarily understood by youngsters with reading difficulties.

2. Language arts and English resources may be too unfamiliar, too difficult, too uninteresting or simply too long. Effective teachers begin with books and magazines with some built-in success: short, not too many words on a page, supported by graphics, and highly motivating. We have learned that non-fiction can be as engaging as fiction in drawing students in. We know that strategies such as building pre-knowledge of the text type or content, reading the selection aloud to the students as they follow along with a copy of the text, interactive discussions at checkpoints along the way when their questions and comments direct the learning, and response activities that ask the reader to revisit and rethink the selection for purposeful, relevant reasons, all can help the struggling reader overcome challenges, and sustain engagement.

    Because it is found on a computer does not make it necessarily understood by youngsters with reading difficulties.

3. Independent reading encompasses the various modes of print, including magazines, graphic novels, comics, newspapers, novels in a series, information books such as *The Guiness Book of Records,* popular commentaries, texts connected to television and films, manuals and instructions, and materials from the Web. Every sixteen-year-old will read the *Driver's Handbook:* we read what matters to us. Teachers may need to provide short, sharp fiction resources, full of action, realistic language, and conflict. Mysteries, parodies, stories with human characters the students' age or slightly older, science fiction — all can play a role in motivating reluctant readers. Biographies of popular sports figures, entertainers and celebrities are often attractive to readers at risk, as are photojournals of contemporary issues.

4. With non-fiction, students value resources with photographs, illustrations, diagrams to help them visualize, connect and engage with the print text. Information books can involve a spread of two pages and resemble the multi-arrangements of computer websites. These students need to see the information laid out in easily read formats, in colour if possible. Headings can be boldfaced and the marginalia can work like newspaper headlines. Non-fiction should be short, "Don't miss this!" Difficult words and terms can be highlighted and explained right on the page. Tables of contents can include visuals, and the index should be clear and concise.

Moving towards Independence

Some have spent a dozen years hiding their incompetencies…

As parents, teachers and administrators, we want to help those students who are having difficulties becoming independent readers and writers; we can refer to them as "dependent" readers and writers, and all of us are responsible for supporting them in their struggle toward degrees of independence with a variety of texts in a multiplicity of contexts. We can begin with the knowledge that students want to learn to read, and we have instructional strategies that can help them. Primary teachers have always known that they were responsible for teaching the beginning phases of reading, but it has surprised, even dismayed, many middle school and secondary school teachers that a large number of their students are still struggling with literacy, in English class as well as in other curriculum areas. Only in recent years have guidelines and support documents been developed for working with these students, and lately, teachers have been sharing their classroom stories of working with dependent and reluctant older readers. These teachers are trying to help their students acquire the literacy abilities necessary for success in school and in their future lives. These students know their own failures in comprehending and composing text; they live with failure every day in subject areas. Some have spent a dozen years hiding their incompetencies, acting as if reading and writing don't matter, missing class, not completing assignments. They feel like failures, and so they behave like failures because they can't read. They become disinterested or defeated. But we can help them grow in literacy competencies — we who are teachers, school leaders and literacy authorities have techniques and strategies that work, that can support their struggles. There is no one cause for the difficulties that struggling readers face. Childhood is complex, and the variables are many. But we do know that, as a literacy community, we can take account of these causes in planning, in program design and in practice. We will find resources to answer their plea of *I Want to Read*. "We want to help you. Sit alongside us and we will begin."

Dependent readers don't know how to make meaning with a particular text on their own. They need support. They may lack the vocabulary or fluency needed to cope with a difficult text; they may be so disheartened that they have given up on most texts, lacking emotional and social confidence; they may not have the necessary cognitive confidence to struggle with either familiar or unrecognized words, lacking a core bank of common words; they may not have any interest or background in the text they are reading, and have little or no opportunity for interacting or participating in talking about what they have read. All of us struggle with reading some types of texts; dependent readers struggle with most texts, even before they meet the words on the page. The goal of literacy is to make the most meaning possible with a particular text in a particular context. Dependent readers will need to work constantly toward literacy success throughout their lives.

Most students who are challenged by most texts require help in several areas of literacy development. However, we need to assess each reader's problems so that we can determine the instructional focus to work on in our scaffolding approach to literacy:

- Is it a problem of not being able to understand the text at a literal level?
- Does the reader lack background information to connect to the text?
- Is it a problem of not being able to read between the lines or to extend the ideas so that the implications of the text are considered?
- Is it a problem of not "hearing" the text in the mind as it is being read, so that the reader never asks himself or herself what is happening, what is going on?
- Is it a problem of not being able to focus on a long or seemingly complicated text, of not knowing how this type of text works, or of never having developed the stamina to read intensively?
- Is it a problem of not having enough of the strategies that good readers use to construct meaning?

- Is it a problem of words — too many difficult words, or a lack of automatically recognizing enough words to push beyond the unfamiliar ones?
- Is it a problem of unsuitable or inappropriate material, either of no interest to the reader, or requiring a strong context in order for the reader to engage with the text?
- Is it a problem of self-defeating behaviour, requiring support and motivation to bring the reading process to life? Have students enough confidence in their ability to read?

How do "good" readers know and implement these strategies for meaning-making with different types of texts?

They know that they read to make meaning. Comprehension isn't just a word on a test; it is the exchange one engages in when interfacing with a text.

- They know that they read to make meaning. Comprehension involves interfacing with a text.
- They connect what they are reading to their own lives, to past experience and knowledge; they relate the text ideas to the relevant contexts of their own lives, and the world.
- They read for a purpose: to be entertained, to find out, to clarify, to extend an assignment, to participate in a discussion. Their reading of the text leads toward further learning; they don't read reading; they read for a reason.
- They use a range of strategies necessary for making the most meaning with the text: predicting as they read along, inferring and summarizing, using previous concepts to connect to the new ones.
- They recognize most words automatically, and use their energy to make meaning, focusing on an unfamiliar word and solving it through context or word patterns. They know when to omit difficult words, and when to return to them when further information has been gleaned from the text.
- They vary their reading rate to match the requirements of the text they are reading, re-reading a part when necessary, skimming and scanning to add to their overall meaning-making of the concepts in the text.
- They question the text, demanding that what they read makes sense in their idea making, challenging ideas or details that don't seem to fit

their personal views, and considering the author and the context of the text.

- They monitor their own understanding of what they are reading, knowing when they have lost focus and become confused, re-reading to get back on track.

- They know how a particular text works, recognizing the features of different types of texts, from introductions and summaries to graphs and charts, to a glossary and index. They use these text features to support their own meaning-making. They read different texts in different ways.

- They choose opportunities to read, practise their literacy and literary skills, become more fluent, more familiar with different types of texts, develop a larger print vocabulary, grow to be more at ease with the process of interacting with texts — in books, on computer screens, in magazines, in school texts, and on tests. They continue to grow as readers by reading widely.

- They are not afraid of the text, knowing what they like or don't like and why, and are able to assess their own interest in and appreciation of what they are reading.

> *Inappropriate instruction may delay or regress a student's growth.*

Supporting Special Needs Students

The factors that explain why these students are "at-risk" or "challenged" are as varied as the students themselves. Some may have medical difficulties, others home difficulties, still others attention deficit difficulties. Some students may learn at a slower rate than their peers, some may experience problems in particular areas, and some may have difficulty in all areas of learning. Some may progress at a "normal" pace, but become blocked with a particular type of text.

Students who are struggling with their reading and writing have diverse needs and abilities. For teachers, this makes working with them complex. One published set of texts, or a series of remedial exercises, alone just can't support the different approaches we will need to use as teachers in designing programs for these students. Inappropriate instruction may delay or regress a student's growth.

- All readers need our time and attention, but troubled readers in particular benefit from individual attention.

- Students in difficulty need to experience what successful literacy events feel like, to know that there is hope for recovery, that they will be supported in their struggle to grow toward independence.

• Students in literacy difficulty need to be recognized for their successes in the processes of reading and writing, to have their authentic accomplishments celebrated. However, this means that they need to have been successful at meaningful activities. Students very quickly identify praise or recognition that is not based on valid achievement.

• We may need to help these students set short-term goals or break the complete task into smaller steps. They will need brief but regular conferences and checkpoints, in order for us to offer support and to provide direction that will move them ahead toward success.

> *After a test, it is useful to stress what the student knew and understood...*

• During sharing times they, too, need to present to the class, and can do so with extra preparation and support. They can show the books they have published, present a book talk about a book they have read and enjoyed, read a poem they have practised, or share excerpts from their journals.

• We need to help these students struggling with reading to learn the problem-solving strategies that proficient readers use to make sense of print experiences.

• We can prepare students for testing situations with demonstrations and mini-lessons. We can often orally direct them to respond to test-like questions, where the pressure to be correct is less than in a testing situation. These little practice sessions can help prepare them for the formal testing events. After a test, it is useful to focus on what the student knew and understood, to build on positive aspects of the experience, and to then move into remedial work.

• We need to spend time with these students individually or, for brief times, in small groups where students share the same level of literacy development. Together, we can read aloud to the students, read with them, and listen to them read to us. We can help readers by giving them a quiet reading time, and by helping them to identify the purpose for reading, and by making obvious the links to their lives that can make the experience with print meaningful and real.

• The school can incorporate struggling readers in peer tutoring programs and cross-age "buddies" reading events, where older students read with readers in earlier grades, and work closely with resource/learning centre teachers.

- Caring and committed community volunteers can often augment the assistance available by coaching and supporting students in their classroom work and homework assignments.
- Struggling and dependent readers can be supported by a telementor, a knowledgeable adult volunteer who, using telecommunications technology, develops and sustains a mentoring relationship with a student where a face-to-face one would be impractical. This can be done using email, conferencing systems, and the telephone.

Building Word Power

At-risk readers need individual attention on word-building activities, as well as numerous chances to apply their reading with real texts.

We need to present words in context, and foster sight-word recognition, since fluent reading requires the automatic knowledge of many words. We can help students build word power by selecting texts that integrate background knowledge. We can then begin to work with the words a student knows to develop strategies for recognizing and analyzing letters, clusters of letters, sound-symbol relationships, onsets and rimes, spelling peculiarities, and complicated or unfamiliar words.

Broadening print vocabulary is key to expanding the reader's world. Students can write personal stories or keep journals, and we can then use their writing to focus their attention on the mechanics of writing, such as punctuation and spelling, and teach mini-lessons drawn from their problems with conventions of print.

> *We can help students build word power by selecting texts that integrate background knowledge and highlight their experiences, feelings, and interests.*

What does a struggling reader and writer look like?

Students who are struggling readers may demonstrate combinations of behaviours, attitudes and abilities at different times and in varying literacy situations.

They often:
- can't bring their personal background information to meaning-making with a particular text;
- can't repair a breakdown in meaning as they read;
- focus on literal interpretation of text instead of inferring, analyzing, synthesizing and extending the reading;
- aren't "hearing" the text when reading silently;

- sub-vocalize as they read silently;
- read all material at the same rate;
- don't see the point of view of the author;
- may present erratic eye movements, have difficulty following a line, or re-read the same word;
- have reversals that continue into older grades;
- have difficulty recalling or recounting information;
- are unable to predict future events in the text, the force that drives us to continue reading;
- falter frequently while reading aloud, often pleading (even silently) for help;
- cannot seem to retell a text;
- don't understand how particular types of text function;
- do not use the text features to make meaning;
- are defeated by the length of the text;
- can't seem to match their interests with any of the books in the classroom;
- cannot select a book, or choose inappropriate books for their interests and abilities;
- have not moved along in the stages of spelling;
- don't understand where to find support for spelling difficult words;
- have great difficulty with handwriting;
- cannot find a topic to write about;
- don't see a reason for editing written work;
- never arrive at the publishing stage of writing;
- are not growing in their use and knowledge of conventions in writing;
- are unable to connect their own written expression with what they have read;
- have difficulty participating in the social aspects of literacy;
- seem unable to respond to the text in group discussions;
- have difficulty in other subject areas that require literacy skills;
- are unable to assess and reflect upon their literacy competence and experiences;
- are learning to read and write in English as a second language, but are already literate in their home language;
- are not using technology to promote their own developing literacy skills;
- avoid reading, or pretend to read.

Reluctant Readers

Reluctant readers are students who can read, but for whatever reason, don't. They may feel inadequate as readers compared to their siblings or to other, more proficient readers in the class. We cannot group all reluctant readers together, for there are many different reasons for their difficulties, many stumbling blocks to their growing as readers: their background experiences; how they feel about themselves as learners; their interests; the context of the classroom (the teacher's skills and attitudes, the resources, the pressures of curriculum).

Kylene Beers classifies these readers in three categories:
- dormant (they like to read,
  but often do not make the time to do it);
- uncommitted (do not like to read,
  but may read in the future);
- unmotivated (do not like to read and do not
  ever expect to change their minds).

Reluctant readers are students who can read, but for whatever reason, don't.

Kylene Beers explains that even proficient and motivated readers become "dormant" at times: on weekends, during holidays, or after a major project. As well, unmotivated readers may see reading time as skill and drill, rather than as a satisfying and pleasurable activity. Often, they have been through remedial situations, special programs, or commercial drill kits, but they have missed the internalized motivation to read. There are strategies and techniques that have a high success rate with discouraged and frustrated youngsters.

We need to help reluctant readers think about what they have read through a variety of response activities. For example, as they connect their reading with their writing, they are learning about both aspects of literacy, strengthening their understanding of the text and making connections with their own worlds of meaning. As they participate in building graphic organizers in the form of webs and charts, they can often see the relationships between the characters in a story or the facts in an information text. The computer can be a great help to these students as they see their words take shape and their ideas appear organized. As well, handwriting difficulties are not evident on computer screens.

As well, handwriting difficulties are not evident on computer screens.

An Example of Intervention — Reading Recovery™

Sometimes, a student requires specialized help, and this process is significant to the student's future success as a reader. Whether the program is inclusive or is based on withdrawal, the teacher will need to be aware of the support the community can offer in assisting young readers in difficulty.

For example, Reading Recovery™ was developed by Marie Clay to help young readers in grades one and two. Its premise is simple — withdraw students who are experiencing serious reading delays and have them work with a specially trained teacher on a one-to-one basis for a 30-minute period each day for a period of 16 weeks. When the student is at a level that is similar to that of the majority of his or her peers, the student no longer needs the program and can return to the regular program.

> *Each student's program is unique and builds on what the student knows.*

The program began in New Zealand and has gained popularity in North America. Assessment of students is one of its cornerstones — students need to be assessed and a thorough understanding of their abilities and knowledge determined before the program begins. Each student's program is unique and builds on what the student knows. Only those students who are considered seriously at risk are eligible for the program.

Reading Recovery™ teachers have special training in reading development. The program that the teacher draws up for each student is centred on using children's books and the student's own stories as the basis for learning. By drawing the student's attention to sound-letter correspondences and letter patterns, the teacher can help the student to explore the connections between oral language and print. A Reading Recovery™ session may include the following components:

- reading a new story;
- making words using magnetic letters;
- writing a story together;
- talking about the story;
- analyzing words and patterns in the story;
- re-reading a story that was read the previous day to allow the teacher to note progress.

Only a small number of students in a school can be accommodated in the Reading Recovery™ teacher's schedule. As well, the student spends the rest of the day with the classroom teacher, and therefore, the student's literacy future is dependent on the bridging of the two programs.

Issues of Gender and Diversity

Schools need to work on issues of diversity in literacy, taking advantage of differences in age, gender, dialect, language and culture, seeing them as advantages for teaching. Emilia Ferreiro, an authority on the relationships between language and literacy, writes in her book *Past and Present of the Verbs to Read and to Write*, "We need to see the contexts for building community between and despite difference."

As teachers, we want to examine the issues pertaining to the literacy lives of boys and girls, how they perceive themselves as readers, and how parents, teachers and peers influence their literacy development. The role of gender in reading success is complex, and we need to uncover many of the assumptions and stereotypes that parents and educators have about boys in particular, and how they handle the world of print texts.

> *The role of gender in reading success is complex...*

The New Gender Gap makes the point that from kindergarten through university, boys are becoming the second sex.

It may still be a man's world. But it is no longer, in any way, a boy's. From his first days in school, an average boy is already developmentally two years behind the girls in reading and writing. Yet he's often expected to learn the same things in the same way in the same amount of time. While every nerve in his body tells him to run, he has to sit still and listen for almost eight hours a day. Biologically, he needs about four recesses a day, but he's lucky if he gets one, since some lawsuit-leery schools have banned them altogether. Hug a girl, and he could be labelled a "toucher" and swiftly suspended — a result of what some say is an increasingly anti-boy culture that pathologizes their behaviour.

If he falls behind, he's apt to be shipped off to Special Ed., where he'll find that more than 70 percent of his classmates are also boys. Squirm, clown, or interrupt, and he is four times as likely to be diagnosed with attention deficit hyperactivity disorder. That often leads to being forced to take Ritalin or risk being expelled, sent to Special Ed. or having parents accused of negligence....

Instead of recommending medication, experts say educators should focus on helping boys feel less like misfits. Experts are designing new developmentally appropriate, child-initiated learning that concentrates on problem-solving, not just test taking. This approach benefits both sexes but especially boys, given that they tend to learn best through action, not just talk. Activities are geared toward the child's interest level and temperament. Boys, for example, can learn math through mucking around in a pond. They can read *Harry Potter* instead of *Little House on the Prairie*, and write about aliens attacking a hospital rather than about how to care for people in the hospital. If they get antsy, they can leave a teacher's lecture and go to an activity centre replete with computers and manipulable objects that support the lesson plan.

Michael Conlin
Business Week , 26 May 2003

How representative is this writer's understanding of the education of boys in our schools today? Is he talking about all boys? Some boys? Most boys? Do schools offer programs for both boys and girls that help transform them as well as educate them? If we believe that all students should have access to the literacy world, how will we ensure that boys and girls see themselves as readers who can handle the requirements of the texts they will want or need to read? Non-readers tell us stories of punishment and pain, where books never metamorphosed into friendly objects, where worksheets and controlled readers caused their reading worlds to turn into dark, unfriendly places.

We don't want to generate or fuel new problems for education and for girls as we explore and even promote programs for boys. There are diverse opinions about the origin and even the nature of the problems that we find inside such a discussion. Most importantly, the education of boys is closely connected to the education of girls, and school attitudes on gender will directly influence both. If we focus on the problems of boys, we do not want to endanger the efforts of many involved in the struggle to bring equity for girls into our society. We need to inquire into the dynamics of how boys and girls construct their gendered literacy lives.

We know that no single category includes all boys or all girls. We don't need to add to the stereotype of classifying all boys' behaviours, tastes and attitudes into one single frame, nor do we want to reinforce the generalities that are often applied to boys. But as we look at studies and reports that examine boys and girls and their learning styles, special interests, their growth patterns and their stages of intellectual development, we do notice differences. These differences are not in all boys or in all girls, but are in enough of them to cause us to reflect about our demands on their young lives.

Those of us who are responsible for educating boys are deeply concerned over the plight of many of them who can't or won't enter the literacy club. But our rules for entry are very strict, and oddly enough, computer skills are seldom part of the qualification. Many boys view themselves as non-readers, labelled by their school failures. At least the faltering test scores have opened up discussion on these issues that concern many teachers and parents. To examine this complex issue, we may need to focus on how gender affects the ways in which boys view themselves as readers and writers. The boys' literacy debate is lined with emotional minefields and requires careful negotiation. Even the terms reveal multiple definitions: *boys, literacy, gender,* and *masculinity*. We need to articulate the arguments clearly.

Socioeconomic factors appear to have as much impact on boys' literacy achievements as gender issues. But we have dozens of examples where boys have every literacy support conceivable and still don't or can't read, spell or write effectively. The media reports too often describe boys as underachieving and educationally disadvantaged. Educator Peter Hill suggests we would be better off if we approached the problems by "targeting poorer students, low achievers, picking up disproportionately more boys in the process."

What it means to be a boy or a girl in school is to a large degree dependent upon the school's culture or the classroom's subculture.

What it means to be a boy or a girl in school is to a large degree dependent upon the school's culture or the classroom's subculture. How the students define the role of masculinity can be affected by literacy classrooms and literacy experiences. If schools encourage a narrow understanding of what masculine behaviour should resemble, then that will have an impact on how boys see themselves and how they are seen by others of both sexes. So much of what boys read, of how they respond in public, of how they capture their thoughts and feelings in writing, is determined by the unwritten, but real, expectations of school life.

We need to explore possibilities for promoting change that celebrate and construct alternative forms of being male in our schools and in our lives. Countering the popular media's images of the world of young males is not the only goal of schooling, of course; however, opening up discussion and offering images of what it means to be male in certain places at certain times should be a focus and a concern for every classroom.

As educators, we do want equity in our classrooms: resources that are bias-free; inclusive and gender-neutral language; and disciplines that welcome the strengths of different individuals. Men and women have experienced the world in different ways for a long time, and the boys and girls we meet in our classrooms come with widely varying life experiences, knowledge and sets of skills. They are also at different developmental stages. We do note, with diverse groups, patterns common to many boys' and girls' behaviours, and the students themselves at very early ages profess clear definitions of what a boy or a girl is. As well, many girls and boys have grown to prefer different subject areas and different learning strategies. In literacy teaching, these factors may cause us to re-evaluate our programs so that boys will view language arts activities as useful or worthwhile, and begin to connect with print-focused learning.

> *"…male and female may mean less today than ever, but they still mean plenty."*

In the article *Boy vs. Girl; Understanding Gender*, it says that "male and female may mean less today than ever, but they still mean plenty."

Young men lead young women in one troubling statistic: 17 percent of them have not completed high school, compared to 13 percent of females. This persistent failure of school to engage some boys is frequently interpreted as a sign that girls are getting all the attention. But who says gender is a zero-sum game, where the advances of one sex come at the expense of the other? The great downfall for many little boys is reading, which makes a recent study on male literacy all the more intriguing.

Kathy Sanford, Assistant Professor of Education at the University of Victoria, and co-author Heather Blair, who holds a similar position at the University of Alberta, tracked a group of elementary boys for two years. Their conclusion: boys aren't the illiterate louts they're made out to be; they're just literate in what interests them, be it sports, computer-gaming websites or collectible cards. There are developmental reasons for this, Sanford says. "Boys develop verbal skills more slowly. They certainly struggle with fine motor skills, which has a huge impact on their ability to read and write, and to sit still and all those kinds of things at an early age."

> By the time boys catch up, they're often "pathologized" as poor readers. Schools, she says, would do well to augment traditional reading materials with items of popular culture, and not just to placate hyper little boys.
>
> *MACLEAN'S*
> 26 May 2003

We want to focus on readers who may be having difficulties— boys and girls who lack success in reading and writing or who see themselves as failures. If we don't help them, they will be unable to participate in most curriculum subjects, often forced to hide their inabilities in unhelpful ways. They may become *fake readers*, or eventually, dropouts. Such students have no "thinking" involvement with the text; they may rely on summaries by the teacher, or copying what others say; they can quickly grow frustrated by a lengthy or complex selection, waiting for the teacher to tell them what to think.

Such students have no "thinking" involvement with the text...

We need to remember that students demonstrate varying behaviours and attitudes in response to different types of texts, depending on the context of the experience — the expectations, the interest, the social situation. Sometimes, they are readers — it depends greatly on what they are asked to read. Since boys in the early years do come to reading more slowly than girls, they are often misdiagnosed, and teacher and parent expectations about their potential are lowered. Boys, when faced with the knowledge that they are poor readers, are less likely to want to improve. Boys who are slow in reading avoid fiction that is "proficiency graded" and tend to go for non-fiction texts with plenty of pictures when given a choice.

Boys with difficulty in reading need to experience what successful literacy events feel like, to know that there is hope for recovery and that they will be supported in their struggle to grow toward independence. They need to see themselves as readers and writers. Very few are unable to master literacy; therefore, we will need to recognize and help many different types of struggling readers and writers, to find out what they can do and build on their competencies, no matter how limited. That will enable them to move forward and recognize that they are indeed improving.

They will also need occasions for talking to others in meaningful ways about what they have read (perhaps through dialogue journals or conferences). They will need to constantly hear about new books and other print resources — significant motivation for finding new selections to increase their reading repertoires.

Boys will need to act upon what they have read, to engage with the ideas and the language they have struggled to understand, so that their comprehension expands and their word power increases. Most of all, though, they need to feel that they own the reading, that the experience was worthwhile, and that it is now part of their world knowledge and their personal literacy life. They need to feel that reading matters to them.

Teacher Dialogue

Questioner: Do you have a point of view about the significance of a male teacher in literacy?

Teacher: Yes I do. My colleagues always laugh when I get a new crop of students who say, "You're more a football coach than an English teacher," and it cracks me up to see that, but it's a judgment. I don't know that there's anything wrong in looking like a football coach and being an English teacher.

Questioner: Can you see why we would want to keep you in literacy classes with male students?

Teacher: They may see that and say, "So English isn't just for girls." In other respects, I might lose a lot of those kids because I operate on a different level than I think a lot of English teachers do. I'll spend a lot more time discussing things than challenging them with texts or hands-on work with reading. I played hockey and football in school, and I play hockey now. I had too much respect for my dad to take any shop classes or tech classes when I was in school. I'm not very adept at fine motor skills, but my dad's an electrician, and he is excellent. He is a perfectionist and I knew there was no way I could measure up to that, so I didn't even try. He was always out tinkering with a car. He's got a Fairlane which I just love; it's a beautiful car. If I have any free time, I should go to the auto class and sit in and learn a little. I can change my oil, change my air filter, but it ends there. And for a lot of the boys I teach, especially my 2P class or my ELS class, that is where they really do their work. They were excellent in the tech class; they were excellent in auto class. They are the ones who are going to be either working on cars, building cars, or building houses.

That's really where they're going to be and they love that.

Questioner: And you can't bring that into your English class? Or is it two solitudes?

Teacher: In the class that I'm talking about, one of the boys who sat at the back of the class and didn't do much took me down one day and showed me everything that needed to be done on my car. I needed a new strut on one side, and so on. He just walked me through everything. The only other person who's ever been so good walking me around a car was my uncle who's a mechanic, and quite a good one. I said to the student, "Josh, here you are worried about getting up and doing a three-minute presentation in class, and you've just walked me through everything that needs to be done on my car for 10 or 15 minutes. You can now go and make that speech!"

Are male role models helpful in promoting literacy with boys who are reluctant or troubled readers? Are we careful in our teaching not to promote stereotypes about us as teachers or boys and girls as students? And is there a danger in attempting to be relevant and sociable that we will leave our students as we met them, lacking specific strategies and techniques that would open their literacy worlds, offer them new options as readers and writers? We need teaching and learning classrooms where our students grow in literacy strengths, while feeling they are in a secure environment, with teachers who are tuned in to their lives, and who also promote a rigorous, involving program.

The following article reports on the fact that men are falling further behind women in earning college degrees, and that many experts fear the social and economic effects of that increasing gap.

> More men who are better educated would add to the skilled-labor force, increase tax revenue, and improve living standards, the report says. That also would reduce the number of children in fatherless homes, lower the prison population, and reduce costs for social services, says lead author Andrew Shum of the Center for Labor Market Studies at Northeastern University in Boston, which prepared the report.
>
> "If you want to understand poverty, the bleak education of men is, I would argue, the most important factor," Shum says....

> The report makes clear that the gender gap, which exists across major racial and ethnic groups, age groups, in nearly every state and among all but the highest income levels, is expected to widen even more.
>
> Mary Beth Marklein
> *USA Today*

Issues of gender and literacy concern the future of both boys and girls. We need to keep in mind that our literacy goals have to work toward equitable programs that meet the needs of all of our students.

English as a Second Language or Dialect

As the racial, ethnic, cultural, and linguistic diversity of a community changes, so do the educational needs of its students. In recent years, the number of students entering our elementary and secondary schools who speak English only as a second language, or who have little proficiency in English, has increased dramatically. In some schools, English as a Second Language/Dialect (ESL/ESD) students make up a majority of the school population.

First, teachers need to realize that it is important to honour each student's culture. By providing an atmosphere where these students see their past experiences as valuable to their learning of English, they have in place a set of skills and a knowledge bank on which they can draw as they learn the language. They may benefit from being able to speak and write in their home language as they become accustomed to their new surroundings.

These readers face a special challenge. Although they share their peers' reading tastes, their level of English precludes them from reading many age-appropriate texts. These students generally do not want to read books that are read by younger students. High-interest, low-vocabulary novels were developed to fill this gap, but did not prove to be a great success because of their general lack of plot and character sophistication. What, then, do teachers use as texts for these students that will appeal to their humour, their sense of adventure and their need for a good story? It is imperative that ESL/ESD readers gain experience with more than just simple texts. By giving these students the same books as others are reading, and then structuring the learning so that they can receive assistance and support as they read, these students can sustain their interest while advancing their literacy skills.

Although students who do not speak English are welcomed into a reception classroom, those of us who have learned a second language know from experience that we do not gain true mastery until we are immersed in the language environment and truly need to communicate. We also know that students placed in the regular classroom as soon as possible will feel part of the community sooner and learn language much faster from real interaction with native speakers. The ESL teacher can then move through the school working with the students and assisting the teachers by offering special strategies for working with ESL students. The Vancouver School Board offers us a useful summary on examining the needs of ESL students, and we draw upon their report to inform our comments.

While we encourage students to integrate with the life of the classroom and the wider community, we have learned that we must give due weight and respect to the first language and cultural background of the students and their families. Multicultural themes are now part of most classroom curricula, and texts in students' first languages are included in classroom libraries so that students are encouraged to think, speak, read, and write in their first language as well as in English.

Interaction with users of English is a major causal variable underlying both the acquisition of English and ESL students' sense of belonging to society. The entire school is therefore responsible for supporting the learning and interactional needs of ESL students, and ESL provision should integrate students into the social and academic mainstream to the extent possible.

The educational and personal experiences ESL/ESD students bring to schools constitute the foundation for all their future learning — schools should therefore attempt to amplify rather than replace these experiences. ESL/ESD students benefit from literacy strategies that build on their oral ability and extend their speaking and listening vocabularies. In this way, they can bring their existing language competency to their print experiences.

Although English conversational skills may be acquired quite rapidly by ESL students, upwards of five years may be required for ESL students to reach a level of academic proficiency in English comparable to their native-English-speaking peers. Schools must therefore be prepared to make a long-term commitment to support the academic development of ESL students.

If ESL students are to catch up academically with their native-English-speaking peers, their cognitive growth and mastery of academic content must continue while English is being learned. Thus the teaching of English as a second language should be integrated with the teaching of other academic content that is appropriate to students' cognitive levels. By the same token, all content teachers are also teachers of language.

The academic and linguistic growth of ESL/ESD students is significantly increased when parents see themselves, and are seen by the school staff, as co-educators of their children along with the school. Schools should therefore actively seek to establish a collaborative relationship with parents from our diverse communities that encourages them to participate with the school in promoting their children's academic progress.

Cross-Cultural Literacies

Our classrooms are rich with the intricacy and multiple dimensions of many cultures and the vibrancy which comes from cross-cultural literacies. Some of our students have had the benefit of growing up with more than one language and cultural lens in their homes. They bring diverse social understandings, expectations and views about life to the dialogues in the school and the classroom. Literacy development in English can be strongly supported by taking full advantage of opportunities for students to share, through their writing and reading choices, and their conversations, who they are and what they value. These literacy explorations serve a dual purpose: first, they provide a fertile field for the growth of language competency in each student. Second, they help all students in the community of the classroom come to know and appreciate different perspectives and to recognize the narrowness of a singular vision of their world or those who inhabit it. In an increasingly global environment, our diverse stories build bridges and close gaps to create a civil society.

Teachers and parents combining efforts to respect the dignity of students with special needs

Respecting the dignity of individual students, especially those with special needs, and forging strong links between the teacher and parents, make reading success possible for students who face challenges. Special Education withdrawal programs for struggling students can have very damaging consequences if they single out students and make them feel stigmatized or inadequate. In the regular classroom and in withdrawal settings, we must avoid rote activities that focus on skills in isolation and call for little engagement or connection to what interests students.

Name of student: Campbell
Grade or Age: Grade 5, Age 10
By: Sarah Burchell

I first met Campbell three years ago. Campbell was an energetic, happy boy who came from a supportive family but he had been having trouble learning to read since he entered school. Campbell's parents provided him with many rich literacy experiences and he had been through Reading Recovery™. His grade 1/2 teacher was a very experienced and successful teacher who ran an excellent program. The school had just undergone a two-year process of having Campbell tested and placed on an Individualized Education Plan (IEP) to ensure he would receive the help that he needed. During the first week of school, I spoke with Campbell's mother, who was apprehensive about how Campbell would succeed with a different teacher.

Like most children, Campbell did not want to stand out. It was important that Campbell feel that the classroom was a safe environment in which he could take risks. I made an extra effort to recognize his successes and be very discreet when making any modifications. As Campbell's comfort level in my classroom increased, he began to take more risks and he became more confident.

Students in my classroom have a lot of choice over what they read, and I use both guided reading and literature circles to keep them engaged. By the end of the year, Campbell had developed a positive attitude toward reading and writing and, despite not receiving much one-on-one literacy instruction at school, he had made progress and his confidence was thriving.

By grade 5, Campbell had made great progress with his reading and had received regular small-group and individual instruction from a Special Education teacher and a classroom assistant. Campbell was very interested in non-fiction and, when reading about topics that interested him, his comprehension was high. Although Campbell is considered to be an "at-risk" student, his literacy world is much broader than many other children who have good reading skills. Campbell still struggles with reading, but I think he is a good example of how, with the right conditions (child, teachers, parents, text), a child can successfully navigate through the literacy landscape.

Academic Struggles Produce Behavioural Problems

Focused instruction through Reading Recovery™ strategies and careful choice of reading materials can capture the struggling reader's interest. In addition, the creation of engaging writing tasks to capitalize on the student's self-identified areas of curiosity were instrumental in helping Allan become proficient in reading and writing. The disruptive behaviour of students who are having academic difficulty is often redirected more positively when they experience success with academic tasks that are designed to connect with the student's personal experience, interests and skill level.

Name of student: Allan
Grade or Age: Grade 1
By: Tania Dawson

Allan was a happy, articulate and very physical child who had great difficulty interacting with peers and fitting into the school environment. He was impulsive, often hurt others, did not appear to have remorse for his actions and was struggling academically.

Suggestions were offered to the teacher about positive reinforcement, behavioural strategies and academic ideas. A follow-up date was set, but a follow-up showed little change. His name was presented at the end of the year as a possible candidate for Reading Recovery™ but, given his December birthday, he was not eligible for the first round in September. The grade one teacher also presented him to the Case Conference Team and, as a result of serious physical incidents, a behavioural plan was developed and put in place. Allan spent a fair amount of time in the office and was, at times, sent home.

By Christmas, Allan was deemed the lowest achieving child in grade 1, which secured his place in Reading Recovery™. As the Reading Recovery™ teacher, I was delighted. During our first few sessions, I discovered Allan's love of the outdoors. His family had a cabin up north where they went on the weekends. He would snowmobile in the winter, dirt bike in the summer, and fish in all seasons. His mother was a veterinarian, and Allan's knowledge of animals was astounding. I'm still not sure which of us learned more when I taught Allan.

Allan, however, continued to have behavioural difficulties in his regular class, which often resulted in his being sent to the school office first thing in the morning. As a result, he was missing many of his classes with me. The plan was eventually modified so that Allan began his morning in my office.

Allan's progress in Reading Recovery™ was slow but steady. His left-handed letter production showed significant fine motor challenges and we discovered that Allan had difficulties with visual motor tracking as a result of an eye condition. When these obstacles were overcome, Allan's enthusiasm and drive prevailed. Allan wrote about what intrigued him and I carefully selected books that would be of interest. Reading on the weekends was hard to fit in, but with diligent parental support, an agreement was reached where Allan would read in the car on the way to and from the cabin. He was particularly taken with the Oxford series in which a little boy Kipper is often in mischief.

As Allan grew in skills, his behaviour became less extreme. He became an avid reader and writer. Last year, his grade 3 teacher proudly sent him to me so he could read the level 30 PM benchmark text and share the Spiderman story he had just written. Both were delightful.

The chicken or the egg?
Failing to learn to read can cause sullen, negative behaviour and
negative behaviour gets in the way of learning ... a vicious circle

Behavioural problems with "at-risk" learners often are the result of dramatic difficulties in their academic efforts. The behavioural manifestations of extreme frustration and inner anguish at failing to learn to read when peers are able to are frequently misunderstood and sometimes these negative behaviour patterns lead to teachers assuming these students can't be taught. Often students have significant strengths in oral language, which can be used to support their breakthrough to literacy. In Sam's case, although his struggle to learn to read is far from over, he can compose intricate stories which can provide rich reading material and a way to extend his sight vocabulary.

Name of Student: Sam
Grade or Age: Grade 2
By: Gwen McCutcheon

Sam attended grade 1 at our school until midway through last year when his erratic and often violent behaviour led to a placement in a small "behaviour" class at another school. Normally, these placements are for a duration of 17 weeks; however, in Sam's case, it was recommended that he return there in the fall of grade 2. Since he was making very limited academic progress, it was also decided that he be assessed by a psychologist. The report indicated a severe learning disability, despite an above-average intelligence. At the end of his term in the special class, the teachers there reported that he was frequently sullen and non-compliant although his violent outbursts had diminished.

The psychologist did not think he would learn to read. At age 7, he did not know the letters of the alphabet. The teachers in the small-class setting believe that he may need a residential treatment program for behavioural maladjustments.

When he returned to our school six weeks ago, one of the first things he did was walk into my office and pick up my story stick. He started to reminisce about the stories I had told from that stick. Sam loves stories, but when I invited him to read with me, he firmly declined, stating

that his father read with him at home. Instead, we began a series of conversations about books we enjoy. Sam recounted long complex fantasy tales, some of them very scary and others quite irreverent.

In view of Sam's reluctance to be instructed in reading and his diagnosed difficulties, I decided to try him on writing. My goal is to move him from his area of strength (oral language) toward his area of weakness (visual memory). He dictates stories to me and I write them down. He has no difficulty with this task, and tackles the composition process eagerly. Talking with this bright, imaginative boy is turning out to be a real pleasure.

After he dictates the story, I re-read it to him and then invite him to join in. He can point to the words with accurate one-to-one correspondence while he re-reads the selection. When I tell him that he is reading, he grins and says: "You always say it first. Then I can read because I keep it in my head." Of course, this is true, and his strong auditory memory is making this process a fairly successful one. However, when I ask Sam to read an individual word in the selection, he can identify it only by re-reading from the beginning with one-to-one correspondence. Visual information seems to give him little support. Once I asked him to attend to the word "likes" in his story. I asked him what letter it started with, and he raised his index finger and said, "The letter that looks like this." After several sessions, it seemed that Sam was beginning to trust me, and feel more confident about the work. At this point, I spread out some large plastic letters and asked if he knew any. He knew four. The "K" was a real puzzler for him, and he suddenly jumped out and said he had to put something away in the classroom. He ran out and came back and told me that the letter was "c." Later, his teacher told me that he had come into the room and asked what made the "c" sound.

Reflections at the six-week point:

1. Clearly, Sam wants to read. He knows the value of print text. Part of his anger and sullen behaviour could be due to the perception that the thing he wants badly is very, very hard for him, and also seemingly very easy for other children, even his own younger brother.

2. Sam is smart and articulate. It is possible that he has the largest listening and speaking vocabulary of any student at my school.

3. It appears that Sam has silently given up on learning how to read. I suspect that this decision has been an anguished one. It is my observation that seven-year-olds who cannot read are in a private hell that they rarely talk about. It is always a mistake to assume they don't know and don't care. They are usually terrified.

4. Every child was asked to bring in a favourite book for a photograph for our literacy board. Sam chose the *Scooby Doo* book from school, rather than any book from home. Like countless other children in our schools, Sam has got the message that the home culture is inferior to the school culture (despite my overt approval of and interest in his home stories).

5. I know that without a means to strengthen his visual memory, Sam will have a great deal of difficulty in learning to read fluently. My job right now is to help him recall some of the key words in his dictated stories, and move him toward identifying them in isolation. I expect that this will work until we get to about 20 words. Then he will need more than just memory to unlock the words. But what? Sounding out words part by part may be the answer, but three years of alphabet and letter-sound awareness has only yielded a recall of four letters.

6. My strategy is to hedge my bets and do two full 30-minute lessons every day with him. One will be a continuation of the language experience work described above. The other will be a systematic progression through the *Oxford Reading Tree* books. These stories have a lot of repeated vocabulary, large print, appealing stories, and continuing characters. Reading Recovery™ children enjoy and progress well with these books.

If Sam enters grade 3 next year as a non-reader, I wonder if any program or teacher will be able to help him. The window for success is closing, and I am very worried about him.

Janet Bright

Facilitator, Literacy Implementation

Halifax Regional School Board, Nova Scotia

Co-ordinates advice and support for P-12 programs

"We work to activate prior knowledge and find out what kids can do."

Literacy strategies that work

- provide a wide range of reading materials and allow students to select books that they can read comfortably on their own;
- activate prior knowledge by pre-reading discussions;
- encourage students to ask questions about the text when they are working in small groups or independently;
- foster both personal responses and critical responses to the text by drawing on students' own experiences as they make sense of the text;
- teach mini-lessons on what good readers do such as visualizing and making connections;
- help students with fluency in reading by emphasizing phrasing, punctuation and effective expression in oral reading;
- provide specific instruction to help students make effective use of text formats such as charts, graphs, bold print, and punctuation as an aid to comprehension;
- provide help with technical terms in non-fiction material to develop understanding before and during reading;
- use technology to link to ideas and extend reading opportunities on topics of interest.

Assessment:

- assess every student individually by an external team, and give feedback to classroom teachers;
- keep running records during the assessments;
- help students self-assess reading skill and comprehension.

Other points to consider:

- when possible, have extra adults in the classroom working with the teacher to help students find appropriate materials; read and discuss content with students, and support students' interpretations with relevant detail.

Professional Perspectives

CHAPTER 5

Teach Me to Read: Strategies for Literacy Success

Constructing Meaning

"We can never read the same text twice."

Our comprehension alters as our life does, as we consider and reconsider our ideas and integrate opinions of others. Our response to a single text changes over time.

> Our compre-
> hension alters
> as our life
> does...

Reading, of course, is more than decoding words; it is more than attempting to second-guess the intent of the author. It is a process of interpretation and negotiation from the view point of our own lives. We need to constantly expand our abilities to process print, from a single word on a billboard to a complicated novel. Texts will continue to present challenges to us for the rest of our reading lives — the words, the language patterns, the structure and organization, our purpose for reading a particular text and, especially, the connections we make.

The reader is part writer. The text furnishes the hints, the clues, the framework, and the reader constructs the meaning. The reader writes the story by bringing self to the print, engaging with the text to create a thoughtful and mindful experience. Comprehension is now viewed as a complex process involving background knowledge, personal experience, thinking processes and responses. Reading shapes and even changes our thinking; reading is thinking.

Some students tell us that they can read the words in the text but they don't seem to understand what they read. As readers, we need to acquire knowledge, explain information, connect it to previous knowledge and then use it in some way. We need to think about not only what we are reading, but what we are learning. As we read, we want to build up our store of knowledge, develop insight, think more deeply and critically, question, interpret and evaluate what we are reading. We construct our own meaning as we make connections, ask questions, make inferences, select important ideas and synthesize our learning. We use the text to stimulate our own thinking so that we can engage with the mind of the writer.

Non-readers, unmotivated readers, reluctant readers and limited readers can all grow with the right set of conditions. We know stories from those who work with adult illiterates in outreach and community-based programs of how their students eventually, and with support, come to be print powerful. We hear, from teachers who work with youngsters in remedial reading classes, of the great strides many students make with guidance and instruction. And we listen to the stories of those who struggled with reading — some of them teachers and writers — who, with the help of someone who understood the reading process, gained membership in what the psycholinguist and literacy author Frank Smith called "the literacy club."

We can base our teaching on sharing the strategies that proficient readers use to comprehend text — showing our students how to think deeply about what they read as they read, helping them move beyond the superficial so they can discover their own ability to understand, to reflect about what they have met in print and to move toward the insight that comes from connecting and considering their connections to the text.

As students grow comfortable using a particular strategy, we can ask them to write about how the strategy works and how it helps their reading. The act of writing about it can make the strategy concrete for the students and allow them to move forward in developing a metacognitive awareness of other strategies to use in their own reading. Because of the complexity of the spectrum of reading difficulties, we need to find ways of supporting and accommodating the instructional needs of the different students with literacy challenges. We need to increase each student's repertoire of literacy strategies.

Students struggling with reading have to learn the problem-solving strategies that proficient readers use to make sense of print experiences. Through explicit instructions during individual conferences and within guided reading time with a group of students, we can demonstrate how these effective strategies work, and support the students in their attempts to begin to incorporate them into their reading. We can refer back to a previous strategy as we introduce a new one, so that the students become familiar with the terms that are being used to facilitate their literacy development.

These students may need extra guidance at the beginning of their reading instruction period to understand the reason for approaching the task at hand, and to make certain they have the appropriate materials for reading and for responding to what they have read, so that they can make good use of their literacy time. It may be helpful to spend a few minutes with them, repeating the instructions or having them repeat them, perhaps reading the first page together or demonstrating the response activity.

Strategies for Reading

- Making Connections
  - Tapping into Background Knowledge
  - Noticing Text Features
  - Identifying Words
  - Monitoring Comprehension during Reading
  - Questioning the Text
  - Making Inferences
  - Visualizing the Text
  - Summarizing the Text
  - Skimming and Scanning
- Determining and Prioritizing Ideas
- Marking and Highlighting the Text
- Analyzing the Text
- Synthesizing Information from the Text
- Interpreting and Appreciating Literature
- Fluency

> *We need to increase each student's repertoire of literacy strategies.*

1. Making Connections

When we are engaged with a book, we bring the sum of our life to the meaning-making experience: our previous experiences; our background knowledge concerning the content; and our connection to other "texts of our lives." We need to help students build bridges between the ideas in the text and their own lives, helping them to access the prior knowledge that is relevant to making meaning with the text. When we help students enhance their reading by activating their own connections, we offer them a reading strategy for life. Today's new knowledge is tomorrow's prior knowledge.

These connections have been classified as text-to-self (connecting to past experiences and background), text-to-text (connecting to other texts in our lives and to the forms those texts take), and text-to-world (connecting to events in the world at large). As the three general categories interconnect and intersect, students have a strategy for coming at a text selection in a variety of ways. As they begin to observe and reflect upon how these connections affect their understanding of a particular text, they can deliberately use each aspect of the connecting frames to increase their personal and collective processes of meaning-making. We can in this way demonstrate that making connections needs to happen as we read, so that we are constantly expanding and processing different types of knowledge.

Before the students begin to read, we can elicit what they already know about the topic or the theme of the book, and list their ideas on a mind-mapping web or a chart. Through guided discussion, we can prompt them to see that they do have connections to call upon that will support their reading events from their own lives, bits of information gleaned from previous experiences with television or magazines, or stories they have heard from friends and relatives. The more prior knowledge we can tap into, the greater the meaning-making that will occur when we read.

> *...we offer them a reading strategy for life.*

We can help students begin to recognize text connections by selecting particular text sets to be used during independent reading or literature circles: books related by common themes or writing styles; books about the same characters or events; several books by the same author or from a particular genre; or different versions of the same story. Often students remember and bring forward past text experiences to clarify or substantiate a present discussion. They reveal that they are using text-to-text connections for deeper learning, tying what they have met before to what they are presently exploring, and expanding their literacy perspectives. We can, of course, model this with our own comments during a class discussion.

2. Tapping into Background Knowledge

Prior knowledge of the topic, previous exposure to the author's work or a personal connection to the theme — all these factors can increase a student's possibilities of making meaning with a particular text. Before students begin to read a text, such as a selection from a curriculum textbook, we can ask, "What do you already know about this topic? " We can sometimes increase their chances of success by providing some background knowledge that relates to the text by viewing films or listening to a story with a similar theme. By recording all their responses as the students brainstorm, we can then have them categorize or classify the information and identify what they want to find out. After reading, students then find a partner with whom they compare lists, and write questions they still need answered.

When students continue reading a selection over several days, a brief review of material they have read may be necessary. We can help them tell the story to the point where the reading ended, write a short summary that they can read aloud, re-read a passage in the text that summarizes recent events, or simply re-read the last page that has been read. We can review aspects of the text, including chapter headings, supportive visual cues and vocabulary that the text contains. This is not to say that we pre-teach vocabulary, rather that we acquaint students with the type of terminology they are about to meet in their reading.

The more prior knowledge we can tap into, the greater the meaning-making that will occur when we read.

3. Noticing Text Features

Students need to be immersed in books of all kinds in order to become proficient readers and writers. As well, they need to receive demonstrations of how books are constructed and used, since books vary in purpose, audience, format and organization, as well as in the publishing devices and designs they employ. Often classrooms with helpful reading and writing programs forget the difficulties inherent in using a single textbook for mathematics or science, or the complexities involved in reading information books from the library. The type of book may influence the language it uses and the way in which information is presented. This, in turn, will influence how the book will be read. Consider how dictionaries, novels, poetry anthologies, diaries and manuals differ. Some books can be read from beginning to end; others will require readers to organize their reading in the following ways:

- scanning a book for a particular item of information;
- referring to a glossary throughout the reading;
- reading part or all of a book to better understand a concept;
- reading part or all of a book to follow directions;
- reading only a portion of a book.

4. Identifying Words

Many words are recognized by students without our help because of impact, rather than sequential teaching: names, brands, ads, heroes and fast food terms to name a few. How can we build on this knowledge base? It would be impossible to learn, one at a time, all the words we will meet in print.

Therefore our brain classifies information about a word we meet in a text, working from the knowledge of word patterns built up from our experiences with print. We want to encourage students to use all the different strategies there are for recognizing and solving unknown words in their reading, long before they begin to read the selection aloud. We need to help students learn how to solve words while reading, not only before meeting the text or after the text has been completed.

We need to be careful of our requests to have students read orally if they don't have an opportunity to explore the text silently beforehand. In reading a text aloud, a student has to pronounce each word while demonstrating through the voice the meaning of the words being read. Unless it is a rehearsed reading, the student may be unable to use a variety of strategies necessary for identifying unfamiliar or difficult words. To decode a word means to be able to say it and understand its meaning in the context of the whole text.

> *We need to be careful of our requests to have students read orally if they don't have an opportunity to explore the text silently beforehand.*

As readers, we expect text to make sense. When it doesn't, for example, when we encounter difficult words, we need to use all the information we have to help us understand the word's meaning and pronunciation. When good readers come across a difficult word, they may skip over it with a view to revisiting it later; they may predict a word's meaning based on context and check back by re-reading the sentence; they may re-read known words around the unknown word, look for roots and word endings as clues or locate sounds within the word. For example, sounding out a word — the usual strategy when a student is having difficulty — often relies on the reader's prior understanding of not each letter, but the letter clusters in order to make meaning.

We can demonstrate self-monitoring strategies in recognizing words that proficient readers use — thinking, predicting, sampling, confirming, self-correcting — by suggesting the following:

- Does that word sound right?
- Does it make sense in the story?
- Skip the word and go on.
- Does the word fit in the sentence?
- Put in a word that makes sense.
- Where have you seen that word before?

- Do you know a word with the same sound in it?
- Now what do you think it is?
- Check the word with the picture or diagram.

5. Monitoring Comprehension during Reading

Traditionally, we assessed students' reading after they finished reading, instead of helping them become aware of what is happening when meaning-making is interrupted, or when they lose track or become confused. During the actual reading time, the content may be daunting, class noises may interfere with their reading, or the period of time may be too long for them to sustain concentration. Even proficient readers have times during reading when they find themselves lost or their mind wandering.

> *To decode a word means to be able to say it and understand its meaning in the context of the whole text.*

> *We read because we are curious about what we will find.*

We all need strategies for repairing a breakdown in understanding while reading; otherwise, we just plough on to the end of the selection, totally confused by what we are reading. Worse still is reading the text and waiting for someone to tell you about what you thought you had read. Instead, readers have to monitor their understanding and attempt to repair any breakdown in meaning-making. Students may need to improve fluency, adjust their reading rate, re-read and, most importantly, increase their reading stamina through sustained engagement with text as they read intensively for a significant period of time. Often, oral reading practice in a group results in little or no comprehension for limited or struggling readers, as they wait their turn and focus only on pronunciation. These students need to employ word-solving strategies as they read silently, and then interpret the words aloud.

Students need to be aware of these self-monitoring strategies as they read:

- checking predictions and forming new ones;
- checking unanswered questions and forming new ones;
- checking comprehension by re-reading;
- skimming and scanning to predict and confirm;
- linking prior knowledge to what they are reading.

6.   Questioning the Text

We read because we are curious about what we will find; we keep reading because of the questions that continue to fill our reading minds. Of course, readers ask questions before they read, as they read, and when they are finished. As we become engaged with a text, questions keep popping up, questions that propel us to predict what will happen next, to challenge the author, to wonder about the context for what is happening, to fit the new information into our world picture. We try to rectify our confusion, filling in missing details, and attempt to fit into a pattern all the bits and pieces that float around our sphere of meaning-making. We continue to read because the author has made us curious, and this constant self-questioning causes us to interact with the text, consciously and subconsciously. As we read on, our questions may change, and the answers we seek may lie outside the print.

We want students to engage in thoughtful considerations about the text and its connections to their lives, not struggle to find the responses they think we want.

Often our most limited readers ask themselves the fewest questions as they read, waiting for us to interrogate them when they have finished the disenfranchising ritual of the prescribed print offering. Flexible and inquiring frames of mind are what we want to foster in all our students. Yet sadly, our most frustrated readers have not learned that confusion is allowed as we read, that in fact authors count on it in order to build the dynamic that compels us to continue reading. And as students grow in their ability to self-question, their understanding of how authors think and of how meaning-makers work increases.

We can begin by showing how we ask questions ourselves throughout the reading experience, demonstrating the process and writing down the questions that come up in a selection we are sharing. This public monitoring of our own reading can often help student readers recognize how interacting with text works, and it may even free some of them from their own restrictive patterns of regarding the text as a frozen maze that seems unsolvable.

Of course, teachers have questions to ask, but they will grow from conversations with the text, from the honest revelations of the students' own concerns, as we try to guide them into deeper interpretations. Now we attempt to ask questions driven by our inquiring dialogue, as we would in a conversation with peers during a book-club session, based on our listening to their interactions rather than on our own scripted agenda. We want students to engage in thoughtful considerations about the text and its connections to their lives, not struggle to find the responses they think we want. Gay Su Pinnell and Irene Fountas, in their book *Guiding Readers and Writers*, support this strategy: "The teacher's questions are a light scaffold that helps students examine text in new ways." We can model and demonstrate how effective questions work, showing the need to listen carefully to others, revisiting points in the text that support a particular comment and supporting effective responses of the students.

7. Making Inferences

As readers or viewers, we make inferences when we go beyond the literal meaning of the text — whether it is a film, a speech or a book — and begin to examine the implied meanings, reading between the lines to hypothesize what the author intended, what he or she was really trying to say and why. When we read, our connections drive us to infer; we struggle to make sense of the text, looking into our minds to explain what isn't on the page, building theories that are more than just the words. We conjecture while we are reading, the information accrues, our ideas are modified, changed or expanded as this new text enters the constructs in our brain. Inferencing allows us to activate our connections at deeper levels, and to negotiate and wonder until further information confirms or expands our initial meaning-making ventures.

> *We create pictures of what the print suggests — making movies in our heads.*

Predictions are inferences that are usually confirmed or altered, but most inferences are open-ended, unresolved, adding to the matrix of our connections. Often we need to dialogue with others to further explore these expanding thoughts, and to become more adept at recognizing the need for digging deeply into the ideas of the text at various natural checkpoints along the way. By designing an activity that encourages inferring, and then helping students to notice the process in action, teachers can demonstrate how to use this strategy in reading. Teachers can choose a picture book to share with the class, and read it aloud, pausing as students reveal the inferences they are making.

8. Visualizing the Text

When we read, a process occurs in which we create pictures of what the print suggests — making movies in our heads. And these images are personal, each one of us building a visual world unlike any other. Reading words causes us to see pictures, which is understandable since words are only symbols, a code for capturing ideas and feelings.

Students can describe images in their minds as they read, jotting them down or discussing them after reading. Reflecting upon the meanings suggested by an artist's illustration can be an effective means of demonstrating visualization and the need to reconsider our thoughts as we learn more. If the reader can't make any pictures from the words in the text, then meaning has been interrupted, and the mind is not imagining what the words are creating. It takes practice to paint mental pictures from the text, but as the reader becomes more adept at visualizing, the ideas in the text grow clearer, and new connections can be made with the reader's background experiences.

9. Summarizing the Text

As a reading strategy, summarizing occurs during the act of reading as well as at the completion. Summarizing is an organizing and reorganizing strategy that allows us to categorize and classify the information we are gathering as readers, so that we can add it to our storehouse of knowledge and memory. We need to constantly connect the new information we garner from the text, and to find a way of making sense of it so that we can assimilate it into our ever-developing construct of knowledge. How would we ever remember the amount of data we receive as we read without systematically adding it to or rejecting it from our schema of understanding?

> *What we do as effective readers is use the strategy of summarizing as we read, getting the gist of the text.*

We summarize constantly as we read, sorting out significant ideas and events and other bits and pieces of information. If we are reading a longer selection or a complex and difficult piece of writing, we need to pause and regroup every so often, coming to grips with a means of classifying the barrage of information we are receiving. We might make notes to help us connect and remember details so that we can focus on the big picture; we might check the table of contents to strengthen our awareness of where a section fits into the whole; we might re-read the introduction to clarify the framework of the information we are meeting. What we do as effective readers is use the strategy of summarizing as we read, getting the gist of the text.

10. Skimming and Scanning

Skimming and scanning are reading strategies students can use when reading for information, when re-reading a text or when deciding whether to read a text. When we skim, we form a general picture of the text, and have a sense of the main ideas. When we scan a text, we have a specific goal in mind. We skim through a text looking for key words, focusing on headings and opening and end paragraphs. Working with computers offers constant opportunities for students in skimming and scanning, as they search, explore, select and scroll down.

11. Determining and Prioritizing Ideas

As readers, we have to read the text, think about it and make conscious decisions about what we need to remember and learn. Sorting significant information from less important information means picking out the main ideas and noticing supporting details. Flagging text can help students begin the lifelong process of learning to notice what is important in a text, to prioritize the information, sort through it for significance, and mark in some way the points they will want to use or remember.

12. Marking and Highlighting the Text

Highlight markers are popular among older students. Unfortunately, these students have had little practice in recognizing what is important and often colour in the entire page. They have had little or no instruction in sifting ideas. Conduct a demonstration in finding and selecting important ideas and supportive details by using copies of a common text and having the students compare their highlighted choices. Cris Tovani and Stephanie Harvey, who brought this technique to our attention, suggest having the students practise by using two colours of markers and highlighting every word: one colour for what they understand and one colour for puzzlements and confusions. In this way, they can begin to distinguish what they know from what they don't understand. They can discuss possible strategies to clear up the difficulty.

Coloured stick-it notes can code prior experiences, thoughts, queries and reflections as we read, modelling a technique that many readers use in their reading lives. At the conclusion of the reading, these stick-it notes can be pasted on a page where the reading/thinking processes can be seen as a whole.

13. Analyzing the Text

Analysis and criticism are connected processes: before we give our opinions, we need to carefully analyze the many aspects of the writer's craft that went into the creating of the work. We can help developing readers gain a deeper understanding of the text they are reading by giving them techniques for considering its effectiveness. As they learn to analyze the particular aspects of a selection, they may come to both appreciate the writer's craft and better understand their own responses to the text. They can begin to step back from the initial experience, to reflect more clearly about its effect on them and how the author conveyed the ideas and the emotions embedded in it. Our goal is not to dissect the selection but to notice how it works, how the author has built the text, whether we are reading an emotion-filled story or a resource containing information.

During guided reading sessions or during literature circles, we can help students move toward a critical interpretation of the text they are sharing. Analysis should be a component of every discussion, as students share their personal responses and connections, raise their concerns and questions, make inferences from the information and talk about different aspects of the content and the style. Readers can move toward a critical appreciation and understanding of the text, as the group members analyze and synthesize the ideas and responses that build cumulatively throughout the session. Each member should feel wiser about the text after the discussion.

> *Analysis and criticism are connected processes...*

14. Synthesizing Information from the Text

As we read, we continually glean new pieces of information from the text, often in random fashion, which we then add to our personal knowledge in order to construct new understandings about the issues we are exploring. Piece by piece, we develop a more complete picture as new information merges with what we already know, and we begin to achieve new insights or change our perspective. We keep the issues and ideas generated by our reading of the text in light of our own lives. When we synthesize, we change what we thought we knew; we expand our personal understanding. We move from recounting the new information into rethinking our own constructs of the world. We synthesize our new learning in order to consider the big ideas that affect our lives. We want to develop readers who construct meaning by summarizing the content and responding personally to what they have read, by reflecting on their process of reading and assimilating these aspects of learning into a holistic understanding of being literate.

Students are often plot victims — they simply recount the sequence of incidents that occurred in a story. The art of the teacher is to move them beyond synopsizing to a fuller consideration of what they have read and thought about. In the past, book reports were often simplistic recountings of plot: "and then he..." "and then she..." We want thoughtful, mindful interpretations and reflections of what students have read. We may be able to demonstrate a better strategy by having students use a double-column approach in their reading journals, for summarizing and synthesizing in writing. For example, they could work with a novel they have just finished reading: on the right, they summarize what happens in the story; on the left, they note their personal responses. The final written product can be a blending of the two columns. This separation and then integration of the two processes may help students notice the differences between summarizing and synthesizing.

> *Students are often plot victims; they simply recount the sequence of incidents that occurred in a story.*

15. Interpreting and Appreciating Literature

We want readers to carefully weigh evidence from a text in order to make a thoughtful decision regarding their own opinions; and to combine textual information with their own background knowledge. They need to draw conclusions and apply logical thought to substantiate their interpretations. We want readers to make and to recognize informed opinions.

We want our students to work toward independence, to develop into life-long readers who see books as friendly objects, who recognize the art of reading as the negotiation between the author and the reader, as Louise Rosenblatt, the authority on reader response, said. How can we help students think carefully about the texts they read, to become aware of how literature works? As teachers, we can begin by providing students with a large quantity, a wide range and a great variety of experiences with the genre of story — all kinds of narratives, including fiction (fairy tales, folk tales, realistic fiction, novels, legends, mysteries, fantasy, adventure), non-fiction (diaries, biographies, encyclopedias, atlases, memoirs), poetry anthologies and picture books. Exposure to a wide range of books offers students the opportunity to learn how authors use language, since the language of literature differs from the language of daily conversations.

16. Fluency

Good readers read fluently — they use phrasing to communicate their meaning. When they read silently, they have the opportunity to interpret the text and add it to their knowledge base, giving them strength when they read orally. Less fluent readers, on the other hand, tend to read at the same speed — no matter what the text — both silently and orally, and to use the same phrasing. In repeated readings, a student practises reading one passage repeatedly until she or he can read it fluently. (This will vary from student to student and depends on the degree of fluency, as well as accuracy.) The benefits of repeated readings are numerous, particularly for at-risk readers, and carry over to other texts that they have not practised, helping to increase fluency, word recognition and comprehension. Texts that lend themselves to this activity include picture books, poems and short stories. Choral speaking, script reading, and preparing a story for sharing with reading buddies offer real reasons for rehearsing a text selection.

We can ask our students to analyze and discuss their own reading strategies at every stage of literacy development:

- Can you review the purpose for reading the selection?
- What tools can you use to handle a difficult text?
- What connections can you make to your own background, life experiences, ideas you have thought about previously or information you have stored, that will help you understand this text?
- How will you keep your attention focused on the reading?
- What tools do you have to construct meaning with the text you are reading?
- When you are stuck, what tools will help you to fix up your meaning?
- What parts of the text will you revisit to help you know how to better understand it?
- Are there too many unknown words blocking your reading? Can you leave some of them out and come back to them after reading the whole selection? Is there a glossary you could use?
- Are there specific questions you can ask the teacher to help with your confusion?
- Can you look for significant details or pieces of information that build a clearer picture of what you are trying to discover?
- Can you look for help or bulleted points before proceeding?

- Can you keep track as you are reading, capturing your thoughts in words in your notebook?
- Can you jot points or puzzlements on sticky-notes as you read along, "pop-ups" to keep you involved in the process of making meaning with the printed text? Can you note brief summaries as you are reading?
- Can you read on? The author may have added information that can help you.
- Can you slow down your reading, or paraphrase a section that you have just read to get the "gist" of it?
- Can you reuse what you already know to think about what is happening and about what might happen next?
- Can you ask a partner for assistance, or the teacher for a mini-conference?
- Can you read the blurb on the back of the cover, re-read the introduction or read ahead to the summary for a clearer map of the territory?
- Can you look for clues to help you figure out what puzzles you — a summary at the end, charts or diagrams, a glossary at the back of the text, illustrations, or the previous chapter?
- Can you use sticky-notes to hold the thinking or the question until there is time for discussion or conferring?
- Can you visualize what's happening in your head — make an instant film?
- Can you check information about the author to see why he or she writes and what he or she writes about?
- Can you use another resource like the computer to clarify or add to your knowledge of the issues in the text?
- Can you jot down two or three points that you have read about in the text, and then use them as directions for what may be happening now?
- Can you draw a diagram or a web of what you think is important in this text?

Often, we can set the context for the selections, offering background information, pointing out unseen "bumps on the road," noting signposts that can give direction, and bits of helpful information. Readers in difficulty require clear and purposeful roadmaps to travel through the different texts of their lives.

Literature circles can engage students in dialogue and exploration with their peers

The social literacy developed as students have conversations about their favourite reading selections sets the stage for enhanced critical literacy skills. When comfortable with others, they dig deeper into the meaning, and gain greater understanding of the text. From their reading, students learn to ask penetrating questions and to make astute observations, both orally and in writing, about what they have read and discussed.

Name of Student: Anja
Grade or Age: Grade 7-8
By: Jama (Sally) Janzen

"What's that you're reading?" Jama asked.
"*An Earthenly Knight*. It's for the book club."
"Book club?"
"Yeah — The Maple Leaf Book Club. A lot of schools have it. It's across Ontario. We're going to have a lunch together at the end of the year and we vote on the best book."
"So, how do you do that? Does everyone read the same books?"
"Yeah...I think. We have to read ten books and then we talk about them."
"Really? How do you know which ones to choose?"
Anja shifted, looking puzzled by what she thought perhaps was common sense. "I read the back cover," she asserted, "and we decide which ones might be good for the group."
"So, what do you like to read, Anja?" Jama asked.

Anja is now reading print text at the appropriate level for grade 7; however, she still has a lot of difficulty with spelling and will often use punctuation incorrectly. She can tell and write a story creatively from her own source of inspiration and life experiences. However, when asked to read a story that she has written, she often adds words or completes sentences as she speaks. If I say, for example, that I don't remember reading the words she has just spoken, she responds, "I know, I know, but it's what I meant to say." She tends to get frustrated when she has to edit and rewrite her work.

Over the past year or two, I have begun to see a vast improvement in her reading of print text. For this reason, I believe her social literacy has improved tremendously. She has found a renewed sense of self-confidence and has, thus, developed a good circle of friends at school. With this social literacy, she has also developed critical literacy skills and asks more questions about why people do the things they do, why some seem to suffer more than others, why certain people are treated unfairly, etc. For example, she showed a lot of compassion and a very empathetic view of slavery and began asking many questions about why it had ever existed and why it continues to exist in various forms. For the school newspaper, she wrote an excerpt on the Amistad, a Spanish slave trading ship of the early 1800s. Her ability to connect ideas and present them clearly in written work is starting to improve; however, as mentioned, spelling is still a great challenge for her.

She now seems to be more enthusiastic, open to others editing her work or helping her in some way, and seems to be happily and diligently pursuing her work. I also find that now, more than ever before, she is beginning to reflect on and discuss problems at school more openly with teachers and at home and, I hope, make some sense out of this infinitely complex and changing world.

Other formats for reading and writing that represent the students' interests and intentions

The breakthrough to literacy often comes when learners' interests and intentions are honoured. In Katy's case, her reluctance to engage with print was overcome when her teacher made the link between her strong interest in scripts and current movies and her reading assignments. When Katy could relate what she was reading to her real-life experiences, her reading improved. Providing children with genuine choices in their reading selections and creating diverse opportunities for them to discuss topics of real interest to them through book talks and literature circles are very effective ways of engaging struggling readers and writers.

Name of Student: Katy
Grade or Age: Grade 4
By: Ronald Iannuzzi

Katy is a ten-year-old student who entered grade 4 this past September as a shy and timid girl. The Special Education teacher said that she experienced difficulty reading traditional print. In fact, at the beginning of the school year, she would be reluctant to read print text aloud or share what she had read with the rest of the class. She seemed to be disengaged and uninterested in the novels we were reading. This shouldn't have come as a surprise to me as the assigned books did not appeal to her interests.

I began to expand my teaching of literacy to include discussions of scripts and current motion pictures. All of a sudden, Katy began to enter into rich dialogue with me and with her peers. She began to relate what we were discussing to her life. As a result of these recent developments, I started to provide my students with more choice regarding what they read. They were also now given an opportunity to share what they had read through "book talks" and "literature circles."

Katy was one of the first students to volunteer to present her book talk. I proceeded to share with her that she seemed to have outgrown her fear of presenting and reading in front of the class. She remarked that she was finally given a chance to read what she wanted rather than what the teacher wanted. It was apparent that she had chosen to read books based on the movies she had seen. In order to further immerse her and the other students into literacy, I allowed students to gather in groups with others who viewed the same movies and read the same books. These became lively literature circles.

Penny Meyer, Primary Teacher
Red Deer Lake School
Foothills School Division
Calgary
Student Population: • 500 students
• relatively homogeneous
• team-teaching

"It is critical for students to have wide choices from good quality fiction and non-fiction in what they read, and choice about what they write."

Literacy strategies that work

- provide a wide range of choice in what students read and write. There is a great need for high interest, non-fiction materials for the primary division;
- use guided reading where students, in reading groups, read orally, talk about the book together, work on specific strategies and then write individual responses;
- help with phono-graphic correspondences in meaningful contexts;
- have students do project-based work:
  (i) have students read fiction and non-fiction around a topic related to the curriculum; develop high interest hands-on tasks related to the topic that students are interested in exploring;
  (ii) get parent volunteers to read material to students if necessary;
  (iii) teach students how to do research on the topic; use the Internet in this by giving students a research page to guide their investigation; help them with the search engine, and incorporate new ideas students have as they conduct their search; encourage students to explore at night on the Internet or in conversation with family and friends to gather more information on their area of interest;
  (iv) have students do presentations with a graphic or arts component, as well as a written component; use technology where applicable;
- use literature circles, where students have a choice of books from a range of difficulty levels. Students read, orally and silently, in a small group, and then complete a variety of activities: summarize a part of the story; draw a picture; extend the story to real life; ask open-ended questions of other students.

Assessment:

- talk to students about different things that can help their writing and give them examples of how to go to the next step (e.g., developing suspense or describing the character);
- develop rubrics with students for different kinds of writing;
- highlight successful writing by working out models of what techniques are in good stories, read examples of what these techniques sound like in literature, and then have students try out techniques first in a group and then individually.

Other points to consider:

- use an "author's chair," where students see themselves as writers and share their work;
- extend parental involvement in reading and writing by asking parents at the beginning of the year to establish a routine of reading ten minutes a night;
- develop a Home Reading Program for students experiencing difficulties where students read at home, record their reading, and discuss it with a reading support teacher at school;
- engage in collaborative writing projects with other classes in the school or other students;
- show the power of print in the real world;
- implement Primary Literacy nights where parents come to hear about reading; have a storyteller for the students.

Professional Perspectives

CHAPTER 6

Uncovering and Discovering Meaning: Responding to Texts

Deepening and Extending Comprehension

Students need opportunities to deepen and expand their understanding of complex and multi-faceted texts in involving ways. However, sometimes students spend more time on their responses to a text than on the act of reading. Nevertheless, through carefully designed response activities, we can nudge them into different and divergent levels of thinking, feeling and learning, bringing more meaning to their reading experience. What we look for in responses to reading are instances where students:

- challenge previous notions they held about issues discussed in the text;
- gain new learning through interacting with others who have shared the same text;
- discover new ways of describing a character or an event in the text;
- check the accuracy of their predictions before and as they read;
- consider their own questions about the text that were answered, and others that remain unanswered;
- review the main themes or concepts of the text;
- think about what they have gained from reading and link it to their existing knowledge;
- question, compare, evaluate and draw conclusions from their reading of the text;
- reflect on the experience of reading the text and incorporate it into their lives;
- represent their interpretations in a different mode, such as poetry.

1. Keeping a Reading Journal

In reading journals, students can record their thoughts and feelings about the books they are reading, as well as keep a list of the books they have read. We often need to write about our thoughts before we can really come to grips with them. The act of revisiting and reconsidering our responses to a text is often possible by reviewing what we have written in our journals. In doing so, we are connecting the processes of reading and writing, formulating thoughtful and personal reactions to what we have read. By keeping a journal during the reading of the text, students can engage in a conversation with the author, record critical interpretations, monitor their own progress and record observations for later use in their writing projects or in a dialogue with the teacher. They may also include sketches or charts that support their responses.

... when they begin to adopt the main roles in the discussion, then we can see authentic evidence of their literary growth.

Journals are useful as well for keeping track of interesting or challenging vocabulary, and can serve to keep track of ideas to write about more fully later. Ideally, students would write in their journals when ideas occur as they read, but it may be necessary to develop this as a useful technique by selecting a time in a guided session for writing, or perhaps having students write an entry during every other reading time.

2. Encouraging Text Talk

We need to model for and demonstrate with students the ways in which we take part in literary discussions, encouraging their participation through prompts and questions during the talk-time, revealing appropriate behaviour with our own responses, and inviting these students into the conversation. For students with difficulty as readers, these events can teach them how effective readers achieve, how meanings accrue through the sharing of ideas and feelings, how by listening and responding they can develop as language users, and how they can grow as meaning-makers by engaging in discussions about books that they have experienced. When these readers in difficulty reveal that they, too, have ideas and thoughts about the text and its connections to the world we share, and when they begin to adopt the main roles in the discussion, then we can see authentic evidence of their literary growth.

3. Telling and Retelling Texts

Retelling helps students activate their immediate recall of what they have heard. Each retelling will be unique. What is revealed in their retellings can give us important information about their understanding of the selection, how they internalized the content and what they remember as significant. They can, of course, write a brief summary or synopsis to use as a basis for oral retelling. When three or four students retell the same story one at a time, and if they are unable to hear each other's versions, they can then compare the different retellings, especially if the retellings have been sound recorded.

4. Representing Responses Visually

Some students who experience difficulty writing their book responses or summarizing their reading may benefit from presenting their material through the use of a graphic organizer.

Some students who experience difficulty writing their book responses or summarizing their reading may benefit from presenting their material through the use of a graphic organizer. This strategy is a way of making sense of the reading rather than an end in itself. It should be a rough draft of the reader's thinking and not a product to be mounted on the wall.

Semantic maps can be used during pre-reading to record students' thoughts about what may be in the text, emerging from a brainstorming or discussion session. The activity focuses on activating prior knowledge and connecting to personal experiences. One way to build a semantic map is to write a word that represents the main idea of the text in the centre of a piece of paper, and then write related categories in squares that are attached to the main word. Students then brainstorm details related to the categories.

Plot organizers provide a visual means for organizing and analyzing events in a story. These organizers help students summarize a plot and understand its organization, and they act as models for students writing their own stories.

5. Reading Orally

We can give students the strategies required by oral reading so that they will approach the process with interest and excitement, accepting the challenge of bringing someone else's words to life. Oral reading of a selection can bring context and words to life only if students have opportunities to prepare, practise and rehearse their reading. When they are comfortable with the text, they can participate in the sharing of it aloud. Whenever possible, we need to try to create situations that call for repeated readings of the same text; familiarity with a text can support a struggling reader's attempts to make more meaning, to acquire word knowledge or to read aloud successfully with a group. Teenagers prefer reading aloud to almost any other method of communication as evidenced by the tapes, CDs and DVDs that they buy in the millions, expecting that the lyrics will be included inside the package so that they feel part of the music-making process. They sing the print aloud.

6. Writing as Readers

We need to increase the time that students struggling with literacy spend in writing, in actually composing and arranging their ideas. They can innovate on the patterns and shapes of stories and poems that they have heard or read. We can use the writing of other authors and of fellow students as models for exploring how writers work and how writing functions. We can present demonstrations of interactive and collaborative shared writing experiences, where we compose together a piece of writing, clarifying aloud how we work as writers, what we need to revise, and how we can strengthen our work.

> *For them, talking about what they may write is a prerequisite for the process of writing...*

As they connect their reading with their writing, they are learning about both aspects of literacy, strengthening their understanding of the text and making connections with their own worlds of meaning. As they participate in building graphic organizers in the form of webs and charts, they can often see the relationships between the characters in a story, or the facts in an information text. The computer can be such a help to these students (if they are made available), as they see their words taking shape and their ideas appearing organized.

We need to take time to respond to their reading journals as we encourage them to develop, suggest new books, share our own writing journey, and elaborate upon their thoughts, so that they will be stimulated to continue their writing about reading.

7. Developing Projects as Literacy Events

Students are reading and writing throughout the day in school. If we take note, we can learn a great deal about their strategies as readers and writers. In-depth projects can demonstrate the students' learning in both content and process, and offer them opportunities for teaching others about what they have discovered. If we want students to develop as readers and writers, it is important to help them set up a system that enables them to experience the learning that grows from a project, so that they acquire skills of handling information.

Students need to write their own researched information using a particular pattern or genre, incorporating the structure of the texts into their own work, constructing and comprehending the genre at the same time. We can help youngsters come to grips with assigned projects and papers, but gradually accumulate the strategies necessary for working with a variety of genres of information. Searching the Internet can provide a rich data bank for locating information.

Research inquiries can lead to a variety of other printed resources: magazine and newspaper articles, manuals and guides, brochures and catalogues.

Students will have real reasons for using references such as the encyclopaedia, all types of dictionaries, maps and atlases, or telephone directories to support and substantiate their investigations. Documents offer special insights for research: letters and diaries, wills, archival photos, vintage books, land deeds and surveys, reproduced or downloaded from the Internet.

Spelling is a complex cognitive process learned over time and bound in with all the other language experiences that change us…

Using the catalogue files at the library, scanning the stacks or conducting a Web search can locate resources that can lead to intensive and deep reading experiences. Fiction is also a research source when investigating an author, issue or historical setting. Comparing picture books or novels read by group members presents a different type of data.

Occasions in which students present their inquiries offer opportunities for both oral communication and written and visual demonstrations of the reading and writing processes in which they have been engaged as researchers. Overhead transparencies, used as literacy tools, can help students carefully consider how they will represent their findings. In some schools, students can move into presentations using the computer. Displays and bulletin boards let other students benefit from the research, and young investigators may want to distribute a guide sheet for observers to note their learning and to ask further questions.

8. Spelling Development

Spelling is a complex cognitive process learned over time and bound in with all the other language experiences that change us — the books we read, the stories we tell, the friends we know. Proficient spellers have a high degree of competency in frequently used words, and find multiple resources for the challenges that occur in writing. In order to become better spellers, students need to raise their word consciousness. The more exposure they have to reading and writing, to the strategies of spelling and to a variety of resources, the more they will reinforce and strengthen their spelling patterns. Research has shown that spelling is developmental and improves over time.

Teachers need to keep the requirements of standard spelling in perspective and assist students in learning to spell with a variety of strategies. Each new piece of information gained about how words work alters the students' existing perceptions of the whole system of spelling in English. Sometimes, students may appear to regress as they misspell words they previously knew, but they may be integrating new information about words into their language background.

Spelling is not just memorization. It involves processes of discovery, categorization and generalization. Spelling is a thinking process. Students learn the patterns, regularities and unique features of spelling as they read, write, play with, and attend to words. To help students grow as spellers, teachers need to draw students' attention to specific patterns or groups of words to help them see rules or generalizations. Struggling spellers need to focus on a small amount of information at a time, especially in examining connections among words and word families, and can benefit from such strategies as mnemonic tricks.

We must remember that word power is cumulative and lifelong…

By organizing mini-lessons and demonstrations that focus on spelling problems students are experiencing (for example, doubling final consonants, adding -ing), teachers can address spelling patterns for the whole class or small groups. This models an approach to solving a problem that can be verbalized and visualized, and students can learn how effective spellers use words. Brief conferences with individual students can help them come to grips with troublesome words or patterns.

Students need to attend to the appearance of words and to check their encoding attempts. As they try to spell words, they often discover the underlying rules of the spelling system. More experienced spellers fix up their mistakes as they go along, correcting those words they already know, rather than waiting until they have finished writing. Students can benefit from learning how to do these quick checks, heightening their ability to know when a word looks right. Spell checkers offer us information to help us notice "typos" and to make more accurate decisions in spelling.

Before teachers tell students how to spell words, they need to ask, "What do you know about this word?" and build on students' knowledge. For example, students can be encouraged to circle words when in doubt. When they return to the words, they can write them over until they look correct. By considering a pattern or generalization that applies, or saying a word slowly and stretching out the sounds, students can learn to picture words in their minds.

We need to build word power with these readers and writers, so that they have an ever-increasing word bank of immediately recognizable words, effective ways to discover unknown words in their reading texts, and useful strategies for spelling words in their writing. They can learn to notice how letters fit together, the patterns involved in word construction, how we can take words apart to discover their inner workings. We must remember that word power is cumulative and lifelong, and aim for significant individual growth from year to year.

9. Punctuation

Punctuation helps translate speech to print and print to speech. Commas, semi-colons, question marks, and periods convey pauses and intonation. During oral reading, when students read aloud dialogue, stories, poems, or favourite excerpts, or from their own writing, they must translate punctuation marks into meaningful oral language. We can help them see where sentences end, where there should be pauses, and how they can show them in their writing. The difficulty that many students have in identifying sentences and putting periods in the right places reflects the fact that the printed sentence does not adequately indicate for them the linguistic structure that defines the unit of meaning. When we discuss reading with students, we can draw attention to the devices an author uses to produce certain effects and the ways in which punctuation is used to alter pace, build suspense, introduce surprise, and list items. Students can experiment with such techniques. When students discuss and share their writing with others, they will become aware of the need for the punctuation marks that indicate questions, surprise, fear, or excitement.

Students learn punctuation marks in the order in which they discover they need them, and they learn to punctuate more effectively through genuine writing rather than through drills and exercises. Quotation marks are often the first punctuation students learn — they use a lot of conversation in their stories. As students compose, revise, and edit their work in conferences with peers and the teacher, they become aware of the value of punctuation in communicating their ideas.

10. Grammar and Usage

Many students arrive at school with rich vocabularies and vivid oral language patterns that may vary considerably from what we have come to know as "Standard English." We need to cherish these usages — but at the same time recognize our responsibility to teach students the form of English used and sanctioned by the wider world. Language is a social activity, but it is also personal. It allows us not only to communicate with others, but also to claim and display membership in particular social and cultural groups. All languages and all dialects have their own forms of grammar and patterns of usage. Successful speakers and writers learn when to use Standard English, informal English, dialects of English, or other languages depending upon the context of the situation. The question is always one of appropriate usage, rather than of correct usage.

Indeed, Standard English is simply another dialect of this powerful language that has spread so far around the world. Since students' usage is influenced by the speech communities in which they live, they will learn the standard "school" dialect in the same way they learned their "home" dialect, and for the same reason — to be a participating member of the speech community. We can immerse students in an environment full of positive Standard English models — our own speech to emulate, books to read or to listen to, poems to join in with, stories to retell or to use as a springboard for writing. None of this labels the students' home dialect wrong or substandard, but rather treats standard speech and writing models as useful extensions of the language repertoire.

There is no evidence that they are helped to speak, write, or think by studying the rules of prescriptive grammar.

Students learn to use language effectively and appropriately through interaction with the people around them, from listening to others read, and from learning about language in the context of their own writing. There is no evidence that they are helped to speak, write, or think by studying the rules of prescriptive grammar. To some extent, students may gain facility in writing and understanding of syntax by practising changing tenses, using synonyms, and making transformations in sentence structure, but, as a general rule, competence is best acquired through the comparisons and corrections that children make in their own writing. For example, students' attention can be drawn to standard language through comparing interesting differences in language patterns, discussing a range of possible usages when problems recur in their writing, and examining appropriate usage by characters in books and in the students' own stories.

They can, if interested, undertake comparative and experimental investigations of their own language by considering the kinds of words that are normally used together or that occur in the same place in a sentence or by studying the ways in which changes in sentence and word structure change meaning. Students seem to learn best when they are given a chance to play with new ways of using language, to make comparisons between usages, and to explore the effects of words, word patterns, and idioms. In writing, however, where usage is more stable and where non-standard forms may be a barrier to effective communication, the teacher should help the students develop standard forms by working from their own writing. By surveying the usage differences that are found in students' speech and writing, the teacher can identify significant problems and build a list of ten to fifteen items to focus on during the year.

> *Many students, especially boys, have been completely rescued by the computer...*

When should the analytical study of grammar begin? In the junior grades, students can identify name words, action words, and describing words — and learn to call them nouns, verbs, and adjectives if they are interested in that sort of classification. Also, if students are familiar with the terminology, it gives them a common language to use with the teacher when discussing their writing. However, few students have sufficient metacognitive awareness of the way they form sentences to comprehend such abstractions as subject and predicate much before they are teenagers, so the formal study of syntax is best left until then. This does not mean that students are not beginning to grasp the fundamentals of what makes a sentence—and perhaps in a more holistic fashion than a grammar textbook would allow. We grow in our knowledge of how language works by using language in significant ways, and by reflecting on how language works in our different modes of communicating. We need common terms and labels to help us talk about the functions of our language, so that we can extend our use and knowledge of language.

11. Handwriting

Handwriting is often a struggle for students with difficulties in literacy, especially boys, leading to frustration and even withdrawal, because they cannot represent their thoughts on paper in ways that promote an easy flow of ideas and communication to others. They are defeated by the mechanical act of writing. Authorities such as Donald Graves tell us that continuous writing through the years will support handwriting improvement, and that maturity will have an effect on how we form our words. Many students, especially boys, have been completely rescued by the computer, and now their handwriting has become legible and uniform because their confidence as communicators has blossomed.

Breakthroughs to literacy can come at all stages of life

The significance of reading to young children as an invitation to lifelong engagement with reading and writing can't be overemphasized. However, it is important to remember that the love of literature and the joy of reading can be discovered later in life. If the conditions are right and the reader is motivated by the material and the impact reading has on the quality of life, literacy skills can grow in people of all ages.

Name of Student: Sarah
Grade or Age: Adult
By: Joanne Aronovitz

At home, Sarah regularly saw her mother read novels and her father read the newspaper. Both her father and grandmother would share stories from their own childhood. Even with the good role modelling at home, Sarah remained uninterested in reading. With an extroverted personality, Sarah always preferred to spend time with friends rather than sink her teeth into a good book.

After high school, Sarah and her family immigrated to Canada in the hope of a bright future. At that time, Sarah had been studying English as a Foreign Language since the fifth grade; therefore, she was coming to her new home with some language skills. While Sarah had the opportunity to attend a college or university, she opted for the work force. She was eager to start making money of her own; however, she did not feel confident of her language skills. Sarah decided to enroll in a French course and then in an English course. Soon after, she got a job as a secretary in a law firm.

A couple of years later, Sarah was married and then had two children. As her children grew, Sarah kept them busy with different activities. Like her own parents, Sarah did not realize the importance of reading to children nor was she aware of the positive impact that reading to children has on them. As it turns out, neither of her children became avid readers. In fact, both of her children rarely recall spending much time reading as a child.

Sarah's literacy and language journey is of great interest to me because Sarah is my mother.

I am happy to share that about ten years ago, my mother started reading novels in Hebrew. She mostly borrowed the books from friends as a way to pass the time. However, over the last few years, my mother started reading novels in English. She notices that her literacy skills have improved; this is evident in the way she communicates. My mother has taken active steps in becoming more proficient with the computer and has even opened her own email account. She regularly visits the library and claims that today she can really focus on what she reads. For her, reading is a therapeutic way of relaxing from the stress of daily living.

Teresa Carleton, Curriculum Leader, Languages (English, Classics, Moderns)
Humberside Collegiate Institute, Toronto District School Board

975 students - High Park area of Toronto
- High academic achievement
- Strong liberal arts focus: French Immersion, Arts, History, Writer's Craft

"Teachers must be passionate about their work with their students if they want students to be engaged. Students must see teachers strive for excellence in their own work, and model the behaviour expected of them through their own dedication, conviction and joy."

Literacy strategies that work

- engage in meaningful pre-writing activities: have students talk about the topic with a small group, do research, conference with the teacher before beginning to work;
- have students do preliminary research on topics to be presented in class to establish a context; for example, if reading "Once upon a time," a short story by South African writer Nadine Gordimer, have students look up apartheid on the Internet so that they will bring background knowledge to their reading;
- have students, especially for large assignments such as an Independent Study Project (ISP), choose material in which they are interested so that they will be engaging in authentic learning activities;
- generate excitement about work-in-progress in class by having students, wherever possible, choose among a variety of types of assignments;
- have students write peer responses to student presentations, focusing on points of connection and what they learned from their classmates' work; students then read their classmates' responses;
- have students regularly talk about their written projects informally in front of the class in order to give the rest of the class an idea of the work that other students are doing;
- publish collections of student writing regularly; when students write short stories, for example, once they are returned, have students do a final editing and polishing; then, collect the stories, do a "Table of Contents" and cover page, and copy for students to read and respond. The most avid reading that students do in class is that of classmates' work.

Assessment:

- allow students the opportunity to redo work; have students conference with the teacher first before redoing work to explain how they are going to improve it;
- use exemplars; keep samples of good student work to use as models;
- have students regularly engage in self-evaluation of pieces of work, both oral and written; guide students' evaluation through questions such as: What worked well? What would you have changed? Did you manage your time well? What other supports might you have accessed?
- be very clear about each assignment: describe the assignment clearly; break down the steps required to complete it, if it is lengthy; give a suggested timeline to follow in completing parts of the assignment; explain how the assignment is going to be marked, including a clear rubric or marking guideline; specify the deadline clearly; describe the steps to take to get assistance if students are having difficulty completing the assignment or completing it on time; give an exemplar, if possible;
- de-emphasize marks; emphasize learning.

Other supports:

- enlist the support of other professionals in the classroom: the administration, the guidance counsellors, the computer teacher, the teacher-librarian; have these people drop by class to see students at work to generate a sense of importance in students about the work that is being done;
- keep parents informed of students' progress and any challenges they are facing; ask their advice.

CHAPTER 7

I Want to Teach: The Literacy Educator

How can we go about discovering what reading material, both print and electronic, will engage, inspire and motivate our students? They will need to make choices in their literacy lives — to take ownership of their reading and writing selves — with opportunities to select some of the books they read, the topics they write about, and the projects they research.

The following joint report by the International Reading Association and the National Middle School Association offers a concise summary of what schools serving young adolescents should provide:

1. ***Continuous reading instruction for all young adolescents***
   Reading instruction must be individually appropriate. Reading strategies and skills are central to the success of the integrated, multidisciplinary middle school curriculum, and every teacher must possess the knowledge and skills to integrate reading instruction across the curriculum. Young adolescents arrive at middle school with a wide range of individual, cultural, ethnic, and linguistic differences that have a significant impact on their reading performance. Providing instruction that is appropriate for each student, therefore, requires well-prepared classroom teachers who integrate individualized reading instruction within their content areas.

2. ***Assessment that informs instruction***
   Assessment plans and measures must show learners their strengths as well as their needs. Adequate assessment measures must be supported by strong informal reading assessments that take place in classrooms and involve both teachers and students in the process.

3. *Ample opportunities to read and discuss reading with others*

   To achieve this goal, schools for young adolescents must have ready access to a wide variety of print and non-print resources that will foster in students independence, confidence, and a lifelong desire to read. All school-based professionals must have sufficient knowledge of reading materials to provide guidance for adolescents in selecting reading materials that are interesting and engaging.

4. *Community time*

   As part of the literacy workshop, the class gathers together, building a community. It is often used to organize — to set the theme for the week, to build a web of ideas for future exploration, or to establish the focus for the work. Sometimes it is devoted to the most traditional of classroom activities: instruction, explanation, and direction.

   Community time is a perfect setting for reading aloud. The teacher may read a chapter from a novel or one of a series of stories in a set, introduce new books or excerpts, talk about authors or illustrators, or relate the books to specific curriculum topics. A story may introduce a theme, go beyond it, or reflect upon it as it is completed.

> *All the members of the class, including the teacher, are part of the community of readers and writers…*

Building a Literacy Classroom

All the members of the class, including the teacher, are part of the community of readers and writers; everyone offers ideas, connections, and suggestions that contribute to the learning of others. We read independently, but our power as literate humans is acquired from the connections we make to the responses of other members of the community. Students will care more about the activities that they feel are their own and will want to invest their time and interest in them. We need students to enter the classroom culture alongside the home culture and the "mall" culture.

It is important to build a classroom community that has an atmosphere of cooperation and respect for all members. Classes focusing on literacy strategies act as a forum for sharing with the students the many facets of literacy: planning the day's schedule, discussing current issues, reading aloud significant literature, presenting interactive mini-lessons on different aspects of reading and writing, sharing student writing that has been taken to the publishing stage, and listening to talks by guests such as authors. We all need support from other teachers down the hall, colleagues in other schools, friends online, students, parents, consultants and reviewers. And so do our students.

All students in a classroom must feel they are part of the reading community. Those who cannot yet read or read successfully need to be encouraged to believe that they can become readers, and be supported in their efforts to achieve their goals. They need all kinds of materials in their classroom to gain access to the world of print, and these resources must connect to the satisfaction of reading. We learn to read in the pursuit of genuine purposes. To build a community of readers, we must create an environment for literacy, not just with print resources, but with support systems that encourage students to see all the evidence of literacy's importance in the signs, symbols and screens they meet every day.

Signposts for Learning

Teaching reading is a shared construction of meaning. We create conditions under which learning can be optimized. When students arrive at school in the morning, we can talk about their home reading, the literacy events in their lives. We can point out the note in their mailbox, or the email on the computer. They may come to realize that we care about who they are and that we want to be involved in their literacy learning. They will see that in our literacy classrooms, everyone and everything matter. They will need to engage in literacy events throughout the day, as we constantly monitor and support them. Predictable routines such as reading and writing workshops will help them develop a sense of security in understanding the day's schedule, and help them to use the classroom procedures as signposts for learning. We can make certain that their tasks are achievable, and let them know that we have high expectations for them and confidence in their ability to succeed. We may need to help these students to set short-term goals or to break the complete task into smaller steps. They will need brief but regular conferences and checkpoints, in order for us to offer support and to provide direction that will move them ahead toward success. These students need to be involved with texts that represent potential success, that present only a few challenges at a time, and with writing activities they can handle with a sense of accomplishment. This will be especially true while working in the content areas, both with what they must read and with the follow-up activities. We need to remember that literacy development can occur with many different kinds of experiences, not just in reading and writing periods.

We must make certain that learners with different strengths and challenges find themselves sitting alongside others in the classroom literacy community who are involved in and excited about learning, so that they have role models for what life in school could be, so that they can begin to understand how successful readers and writers function. We have seen older students become "buddy" readers with younger students, and have watched as these mentors began to see themselves as those who can read, who have power with print, and who can communicate with others. A sense of despair can inhibit or even prohibit literacy growth. There will be occasions when teachers will want to work with a small group of students who are having difficulties, but for the rest of the day, we need to make literacy events social and communicative experiences, where readers of mixed abilities are interacting with satisfaction alongside their companions. Students having reading difficulties need to see themselves and to be seen by their classmates as contributing members of the classroom community. During sharing times, they, too, need to present to the class, and can do so with extra preparation and support. They need to share the books they have published, to present a talk about a book they have read and enjoyed, to read a poem they have practised, or to share excerpts from their journals. They can introduce or thank a speaker, review a film that they saw, or demonstrate an experiment with their group.

Planning Together

Organizing a literacy-based program that implements the most effective strategies for helping students learn demands, in the first place, a flexible approach to timetabling. Large blocks of time allow students to conduct sustained investigations, both singly and with others. The teacher and students also need time for planning together. As students take on responsibility for classroom routines, they begin to direct their energy toward tasks and activities. Their teachers are then able to spend periods of time with individual students, giving assistance when it is really needed.

The answer may lie in a reorganization of not only time but also of our own resources. Some things we expect to do need not be done at all or can be done as well, or better, by others, such as the students themselves. Rather than working primarily in a whole-class instruction mode from the front of the room, we can invest significant time in guiding students in small groups, conferring with individuals, and observing them at work. We can use preparation time for more than organizing elaborate lessons that will never run as planned; we can plan units and themes that integrate various aspects of language growth; we can share ideas with other teachers; we can have the students help organize the day so that their responsibility will free us for other duties; we can use "buddies" — students from other classes — and senior citizen or parent volunteers to enrich and supplement the time we can spend with individuals and small groups; we can have students presenting their own research to the class as knowledgeable experts; we can take the time to read to our students, taking them to distant places and unusual times. We have to recognize what truly matters in the classroom and how we can make the time for true teaching and learning situations. Rather than "covering the curriculum," we should be helping the students to "uncover" and connect it to a broad world of learning opportunities.

A sense of despair can inhibit or even prohibit literacy growth.

The important thing about organizing time is that the students should know what to expect and what is expected of them. In this sense, organization is a vital component of a successful learning environment. Setting up a literacy-based classroom can be achieved only with the understanding and cooperation of the students. A well-organized classroom creates contexts in which students want to get work done. They require careful support and guidance until they accept the ground rules and can work at ease in situations that they help determine.

As teachers, we can select resources carefully, so that students at risk can meet moderate challenges in the text they are processing:

- We can create a tolerable level of accessibility with a text through encouragement and feedback.
- We can be careful not to lose the momentum of the reading experience.
- We can try never to leave the learner lost in the complexity of a difficult text.
- We can remember to step back to clarify what type of help to offer.
- We can negotiate manageable challenges with the students, and phase out our support as quickly as possible.
- We can help in directed teaching situations. It is better to learn with help than to flounder on your own. Often, electronically based computer mastery drills masquerade as tutoring but really fail to assist students in developing independent literacy skills.
- We can find ways to support "help refusers" — strugglers who can't self-correct, who don't seek help, who can't regulate their own learning. Lower achievers usually seek less help from us.

- We need effective teaching, but we also need affective teaching, where all the brain's faculties, including emotion, are involved in making meaning with printed text. We need to be aware of how the brain organizes and processes information. Brain functioning is social, emotional and cognitive. Learning is enhanced by emotional connections. Since emotions and thoughts interact with and shape each other, they cannot be separated. Learning to read and write is a constructive process, and emotional connections control what can happen. Students who feel terrible about themselves are often unable to learn.

1. Reading to the Class

Young adolescents still need to listen to stories. When adults share literature aloud, they reveal their literary choices, demonstrate their appreciation and taste, and bring alive the words on the page. The impact will influence what young people choose to read and expose them to books they might not choose or are unable to read on their own. When we read aloud, the shared experience binds the group together in a moment of growth in which the book, the story, and the author form the focus for feelings and responses. We read aloud what we've written ourselves — excerpts from stories that we loved or wondered about, words that touch us or puzzle us, tales from before, now, and hereafter, episodes from people's lives, poems that cry out for voices in the air, letters from friends, stories about places where we have never wandered. We read short stories and long stories in chapters that build up the tension for days. We read liner notes from CDs, blurbs about writers from book jackets, titles, and reviews. We fill the classroom with the words of our ancestors, our friends, our researchers, our journalists, our ad writers, our novelists, our poets, our records, our native people.

> *The important thing about organizing time is that the students should know what to expect and what is expected of them.*

As teachers, we can contribute to the sense of community by reading aloud to the class, often, materials they normally would not experience. When we choose texts that support a theme, we can extend the students' learning; when we read newspaper and magazine articles, we can model how to handle content information. Sometimes, we can have each group discuss a different aspect of the text, creating a real reason for the sharing afterwards. Working with one group in a fishbowl demonstration can help students see how text conversations work. After the experience, we can analyze the process with the students so that they can understand the learning that occurred.

Having everyone silently read the same novel can also be beneficial if used occasionally and as a demonstration of how literature groups can function. Teachers can select a book that most students can read, or offer support to struggling readers, such as having them listen to a recorded version first. This type of activity is a community-building event, where time should be taken to incorporate a variety of response modes into the work. We especially need to read aloud to struggling readers, to increase the satisfaction and joy that quality literature can offer, to increase their background knowledge, and challenge their minds with ideas and constructs they may not as yet find in their own reading. As well, their listening vocabulary will continue to expand, as will the text structures and genres they meet in the future.

The community of learners can benefit from this shared literary experience in a thousand ways.

As teachers read aloud, we become models of how to read, in phrasing, characterization, dialogue, and nuance, and demonstrate how texts can hold rich meaning. As they listen, the students will create their own stories in their minds. We can read several short stories on some occasions, and on others, share longer, continuous stories. Some stories work for all ages; some have special relevance for particular groups: students with special backgrounds, various book experiences, differing sensibilities. Some stories are most effective when read to a small, intimate group; others are better with large audiences. Matching text to audience is an artistic skill honed through practice. A record of what teachers read themselves may help teachers develop a read-aloud program in their classroom and plan suitable read-aloud stories at different levels in their school.

Our students need to know how much there is to read in their lives. In his book *Reading Reasons*, Kelly Gallagher suggests incorporating the reading minute each day:

> *In one minute of a classroom's timing, the teacher (or a student) can read an excerpt from a book or a magazine that represents peaceful writing, a puzzlement, troublesome items, a challenge, a controversy or humorous moment, a quotation, a comic strip or political cartoon.*

The community of learners can benefit from this shared literary experience in a thousand ways. Sometimes a careful introduction will set the time, place, or mood. Sometimes the story will fit inside an existing thematic unit. The teacher can work with the class after the story, extending and exploring the issues contained inside and outside it. By bringing the words to life with our voices, we offer our students resources they might never meet on their own, and we add our interpretations of texts to their literary repertoires.

We can talk about books we have enjoyed in our own lives, and present book talks featuring titles that these struggling readers will be able to handle. We can share memorable poems and songs that invite the students to join in; we can demonstrate our practical imaginative use of the Internet, allowing them to participate as full members of the reading community. We breathe life into printed texts with our students, and our voices connect us to the power of language in our lives.

2. Demonstrating Reading Strategies

How do we help dependent readers approach a text with strategies that will promote comprehension, at a literal level and beyond?

> *We know as teachers that groups are a necessary component of any classroom...*

- We need to give dependent readers direct and explicit instructions in handling different texts, and practice in how effective readers read. They need to see how reading works. They need to know how they read what they read.
- We need to model and demonstrate for these students how we as literate adults come to understand what we are reading, thinking aloud as we share our reading strategies with students who have a copy of what we are reading.

This type of modelling or demonstration helps the students to connect what they are studying to the opportunities of the curriculum in contemporary situations, but, more importantly, the teacher is exploring literacy in action, making meaning together with the students as they talk about a shared text — clarifying, modifying, questioning, informing and rethinking initial thoughts. The teacher could share an article of high interest on an overhead transparency or an electronic slide with the class, noting expressions and words as the students comment on them, pointing out the ways in which certain strategies clarify meaning. We need to model our thinking about processing text out loud with our students, so that they can see how readers work to understand printed text. The strategies we use need to be transparent; the students are learning the secrets of effective readers.

3. Grouping Students for Literacy

We know as teachers that groups are a necessary component of any classroom — as much as we would like, it is virtually impossible to organize and maintain completely individualized literacy programs. As well, peer groups are a strong motivating force in supporting a literate classroom. However, we also know that traditional reading groups based on ability do not benefit students, particularly those who are experiencing difficulty. We need to devise a way in which the needs of all students are met and their development fostered — throughout their school years we want to protect students from the less than beneficial aspects of traditional grouping based strictly on reading level.

A supportive atmosphere is crucial to guided reading...

Classrooms with 25 or 30 students need opportunities for group work in building literacy strategies. Most classes need to learn how to work in groups, the expectations, the strategies for functioning, the checkpoints that support and direct the conversations, and receive feedback and engage in sharing times. Often, guide sheets framing the activity can keep a group on track, and can be used when the groups come together as sources for commentary and modifying and clarifying opinions.

As group members, students can develop their skills of communication and cooperation. They can learn from one another's experiences, and pool their interpretations of text to increase one another's comprehension. They develop respect for their classmates and their points of view and they improve problem-solving and decision-making strategies. For students learning to read or who are having difficulty reading, we can group and regroup students for short periods where, with peers who share similar reading skills, they focus on an applicable topic or skill.

Readers in difficulty have many more opportunities to speak and to interact with text when they work in groups than they do when they work as a whole class. As groups learn to work together on the text tasks, these students become real participants in literacy events, noting how others work with and respond to texts. They are learning how reading works. Cooperative learning strategies are excellent tools for developing and improving group activities and literacy practices, and encouraging individuals to take the perspectives of others and clearly articulate their own.

4. Guided Reading Instruction

Guided reading involves grouping students who have similar reading abilities or who need to acquire similar strategies for reading success. Unlike traditional reading groups, where membership is static, guided reading groups reform constantly throughout the year. The goal of these approaches is to have all students read increasingly sophisticated texts — fiction and non-fiction alike — and develop strategies they can use independently. A supportive atmosphere is crucial to guided reading, as are ongoing observation and assessment. Students understand that throughout the day, groups will be dynamic and that they will work in a variety of configurations. As students progress, guided reading activities should develop into literature circles and discussions of texts.

Guided reading sessions present opportunities for us, as teachers, to capitalize on teachable moments and to guide and observe the students as they are becoming strategic readers and writers. Many reluctant readers can benefit from carefully directed group reading activities, where what they read matters, and how they read is the basis of the next steps in our teaching.

We need to organize guided reading sessions, as frequently as possible, for struggling readers where they can practise using the reading strategies we have modelled, while we work alongside them as a side coach and instructor. The goal with all of our reading instruction is not to teach students to answer questions about one text, but to learn to use the strategies they will need to handle the variety of texts they will meet in school and in life. As teachers, we need to observe and listen to the students as they explore the issues and ideas in the text, so that we can offer suggestions that promote reading success. Sometimes we need to focus directly on a particular strategy with the students, as they build their repertoires of tools for literacy growth.

Students require help to build meaning as they are reading. In a guided reading session, we mediate the reading with what we call checkpoints. By asking a question or offering a comment on what has been read, the students and the teacher can model how the effective reader monitors his or her reading throughout the process. Students can talk about their own confusions, their predictions, their questions, the connections they are making.

We also need to help these readers accept a useful tool in making sense of what they have read. They may think that effective readers understand a text on the first readthrough, and we can show them how we re-read sections or passages or even sentences, to clarify or solve the puzzles that have arisen. If a reader loses concentration, becomes distracted or confused, he or she re-reads to start the meaning-making. After all, students often see a film a second time, a television sitcom a dozen times, and they may learn to read a significant book several times.

Too often, struggling readers are only involved in reading aloud, a slower process than silent reading, focusing only on pronouncing the words, making it more difficult to understand and to remember what is happening in the text. We need to promote fluency in reading for the most understanding to occur, both when reading silently and orally.

5.　Literature Circles

We also need to help these readers accept re-reading as a useful tool in making sense of what they have read.

While in the past students in literacy difficulty were often drilled with worksheets, we recognize that these students require experiences with the "big ideas" that appropriate resources can offer. By participating in literature circles, they can focus on the themes and issues, as well as the words and structures, of the best books for young people. The groups should be of mixed ability, with the students selecting the books they want to read from the classroom or school library collections. We may have to assist these readers with their choices. A wide range of suitable and appropriate books, or selections in anthologies, is important, so that we can accommodate the various stages of literacy development in our classroom. Sometimes we can arrange to have those less able readers listen to the book on tape beforehand, or we read aloud to the group, so that they can enter the discussion as full-fledged members of the group. Models that demonstrate for these students the way in which we take part in literary discussions are helpful in encouraging their participation through prompts and questions during the literature circle.

During the talk-time, we can model appropriate behaviour with our own responses and invite these students into the conversation. When these readers in difficulty reveal that they, too, have ideas and thoughts about the text and its connections to the world we share, and when they begin to adopt main roles in the discussion, then we can see authentic evidence of their literacy growth and they can see themselves as real readers.

6.　Independent Reading

For struggling readers especially, independent reading time during school hours is a necessity for enhancing reading abilities and for encouraging a positive attitude toward books and reading. Providing suitable resources is the first hurdle; then, we need to support the actual silent reading of the text by these students, sitting nearby or chatting quietly to them at appropriate checkpoints to clarify what is happening in the story.

During independent reading sessions, we need to encourage students to read at their own pace, using materials they have chosen. Independent reading sessions should include the following:

- Students choosing the material they want to read. As teachers, we can give advice and help if asked, but it is up to the students to decide what they will read from a selected (and sometimes pre-selected by the teacher) repertoire of resources. Students need to be able to select from quality literature, fiction and non-fiction alike. We do not select their texts, but we can help to ensure their choices are appropriate and meaningful.

> *…independent reading time during school hours is a necessity for enhancing reading abilities…*

- Opportunities to read in class time. Since reading levels are dependent in large part on the time and opportunity to read, we must provide time in class, particularly for students who are not reading at home.
- Students reading at their own pace.
- Help available when students require it. Our assistance can take a variety of forms, from conferences to a small-group demonstrations.
- Brief conferences with the teacher about their reading.
- Recording in their journals books they have read, their reactions to the books, observations they have made during reading, words they have learned, and how they've responded to their reading.

> *We want them to learn how to read, how to make meaning with text…*

Reading for a Purpose

Effective readers have internalized their reasons for reading a particular text. Struggling readers too often read without understanding what is happening. They escape the meaning-making process by pretending, asking someone for the answer, or just opting out. If they are given an instructional purpose for reading the text, they have hope for keeping in mind why and how they should handle the text. The purpose can never be to get through the text, but rather to gain some meaning, some understanding from the process. Staring at the pages because they have to is far different from tackling the text for a reason.

When we ask students to read a text in any curriculum area, we want them to become engaged in thinking about what they are reading as they are reading, not racing through to get to the question at the end. We want them to learn how to read, how to make meaning with text — the words, the sentences, the diagrams, the images, the format, the content (the ideas, the feelings, the issues, the opinion, the information), the characteristics of the genre, how and why the selection exists, and to make sense of it from their own lives and backgrounds, so that they can add to and enrich their understandings. We teach reading to develop thoughtful, mindful readers with flexible and inquiring frames of mind. We use a selection today to teach students to read other selections for the rest of their lives. We teach them how to read both what they will want to and what they will be required to read in their encounters in school and in their daily lives.

Identifying the purpose for reading is the foremost strategy in handling texts that are required reading. Readers with limitations often need to see the parameters of what they will be tackling.

> *All of us are forced, by a variety of contexts, to read what we label as boring or uninteresting...*

• Are they reading a novel in order to write a book report, or reading to enjoy and appreciate the text?

• Can they re-read sections of the novel in order to respond for specific reasons — a character study, or an opinion piece about a significant issue?

• Can they read three poems as authentic readers, and select the one that they enjoyed the most? Can they then begin to note the reasons for their choice — looking into the words and style that give form to the feelings and ideas?

• Can they review the mathematical concepts that underlie the questions they will have to answer?

• Can they see how the information in the essay will add to the structure of their knowledge about the topic, just as the picture on the box of Lego toys directs us in our building?

• Can they realize the need for reading a script silently first, and then discuss it before they are asked to bring it to life orally?

• Can they talk about the newspaper columnist whose work they are to read, to understand the columnist's general views, and the type of column he or she usually writes, before reading a selection?

Instructional support can promote the students' ability to access complex texts. They need to learn how to locate the essential information and not be overwhelmed by the amount of detail or by the length of the paragraph or page. Knowing the purpose for their reading, or even better, why the text was written, can help a reader in difficulty recognize the need for the roadmaps, so that they can negotiate these tricky turns.

A Reading Roadmap for What We have to Read

How do we help students read difficult texts — texts they would not choose to read, texts used as tests, texts required by jobs or government or contracts? All of us are forced by a variety of contexts to read what we label as boring or uninteresting, but we need to complete the tasks because they will in some way benefit our lives. For example, few people like reading the insurance policy terms in the contract they sign, but they need to know what they have agreed to and what they can expect if calamity strikes. Students need a similar purpose for reading what we assign. They need to know how to focus on the reading process, what they will be expected to do with what they find when they are finished, and how to handle the type of text they are required to read — instructions, letters, narratives or information. If the text seems unfamiliar, or disconnected from their previous understanding of the issue, if it's full of different words or terms, then we need to help them find ways to handle what they are required to understand. They need a reading roadmap to know how effective readers read.

They need a reading roadmap.

We can help students learn how to process difficult or required text:

- We can help them scan the "map of the text" — the title and subtitles, the genre, the format — to know where they are heading, to get an overview of the text territory.
- We want them to talk back to the text, question it, interrogate the author, re-read bits, skim and scan to find what is necessary to know.
- We want them to know as much as possible about the author (or the originator of the text). Do they know other texts written by this author, or similar genres that can inform them about the intent of the text?

If we want our students to construct meaning as they read texts in different curriculum areas, we need to give them either accessible texts, or strategies for handling difficult texts. For students who have trouble with the concepts they have to read, with the vocabulary and terms used, with the number of words on a page or the length of the chapter or book, they feel defeated before they begin to read. But if the text is engagingly designed, of high interest, well written and appropriately matched to the reading levels of the students, then learning can begin. How much have they read in the past, and what strategies are they able to use now? Do students who are constantly faced with texts that are too difficult decide reading isn't worth it, and does school literacy seem impossible?

One of the ironies concerning literacy and struggling readers is that they spend less time reading than their able peers, when authorities such as Richard Arlington claim these students need at least twice as much time engaged in reading and writing. As students enter higher grades, the opportunities for extended and extensive reading times lessen, and we all simply have to work harder to create spaces for literacy practice or the students will remain low-performing readers.

Two other factors in addition to sufficient time support growth in students' literacy abilities: providing resources they can read successfully, so that their fluency improves and their confidence increases; and providing effective instruction alongside their reading, using the texts they have read, in order to monitor their comprehension and to focus useful strategies for them to incorporate into their processing of text.

> *Students in difficulty need to read meaningful, authentic texts as frequently as possible, texts of all kinds, especially accessible and interesting books, magazines, and newspaper articles of high interest to young readers.*

What Students Read

Students in difficulty need to read meaningful, authentic texts as frequently as possible, texts of all kinds, especially accessible and interesting books, magazines, and newspaper articles of high interest to young readers. We will need to ensure that our classrooms are full of a variety of print and screen resources, including extensive selections for these special-needs students, so that they can read more and more. Obviously, a reading environment must include not just a range of types of texts and genres from many cultures, but also old favourites to be dipped into again, books about students' current interests, and reading that is challenging but still within their grasp.

In this setting, students must have plenty of opportunities to read. Too often, these students are relegated to spending their time doing everything but reading, practising decontextualized skill activities on worksheets and in workbooks that are not directly connected to what they have read, missing the reading strategies necessary for comprehending texts. These students above all need to understand how texts work, to feel the satisfaction that can come from effective meaning-making experiences with the medium of print or online texts, and to begin to see themselves as actual readers and writers, engaged in literacy learning for good reason.

Classroom Libraries

We need to provide a wide resource of different types of texts that are of high interest to reluctant or dependent readers. If we want these students to read, then we need texts they will want to read, or that with some support and direction, they will read. We may need to change what we think students should read and move them toward these texts by beginning with what they might read, can read and will read. For many, previous attitudes toward books and other print resources have to be altered. One of the most effective means of turning these students around is to fill their school lives with all types of printed texts, and at the same time, the valuable resources of the computer and the Internet. Some selections will work with everyone within the classroom community, some will be effective in small groups, and others will fill the need for individual choice. What is appropriate and accessible to one student may not work with another, and this determines the need for a wide-ranging classroom collection and technological resources. The school library can be a great asset and a revelation to many students for whom reading was previously a non-activity.

> *If we want to improve reading with students in need, a variety of resources are required.*

Sets of novels for groups can often be borrowed from a central book resource, or shared by different classrooms. Magazines are easily collected from households, once they have been read, and day-old newspapers are often supplied by distributors. If we want to improve reading with students in need, a variety of resources are required. There is no other alternative. We know that teachers want their classrooms full of first-rate materials, real books and resources, and technological tools.

Novels

In some classrooms, students who have had great challenges as readers can select novels that motivate them, contemporary narratives that can connect to their lives and to the issues that surround them: Jeff Wilhelm in *You Gotta Be the Book* chronicles activity-based programs with students who became involved in the fictional lives and events of the popular books in the classroom library, and through activities that drew them into the text, found satisfaction in reading novels for the first time in their school lives. When we work with required novels from the past, often termed classics, we need to prepare and support our students for the difficulties that may cause, connecting them to film versions or taped readings. In her book *The Yellow Brick Roads*, Janet Allen advocates the teacher reading the text aloud while students follow along with their own copies, listening to the words read by the teacher with power and seeing them at the same time. We need to bring the option of reading these extended texts to our students, so that their repertoire grows through satisfactory, even enjoyable, literacy experiences.

Textbooks

How are they selected? (Is there student input)? Are they written at an appropriate reading level? Do they represent the newest information? Are they manuals or summaries of the curriculum issues? Do they have supportive elements — interest boxes, diagrams, graphics, introductions, summaries? Are they used as the complete program or as supportive elements in guiding the students? Do they work with readers at risk?

> *Difficult concepts can be explored before the text is introduced.*

Curriculum materials count as reading opportunities, but teachers may have to adapt them, select only portions of the text, or offer support through partner reading or tapes. As well, different subject areas are supported by other texts which extend the content or the issues: journal articles, newspaper clippings, computer downloads, charts, interviews, bulletins, editorials, books, and reviews. By understanding the purpose of reading what they are required to process, and by incorporating strategies that they now can handle, students can work through printed texts that they might have avoided or rejected in the past. They become more confident and competent with positive literacy experiences.

Tests and Exams

Are tests and examinations tools for teaching assessments or for reporting evaluation? Do students understand the purpose of the test or exam? Have they practised using the format or answering the type of question beforehand? Do they see the value of the assessment tool in helping them know what strategy to develop further? Do they understand how the types of questions work, what is being asked for, how to organize their answers? Have they practised reading different kinds of instructions? Do they keep track of their tests, so that they can recognize their progress? Are tests connected to the curriculum? Do students have opportunities to compare their performances to exemplars of successful work done by others?

Information Texts

Struggling readers usually need special support with information texts to learn to recognize the features of different genres of texts, and how to make sense of the content effectively and efficiently. Often, classrooms with helpful reading and writing programs forget the difficulties inherent in using a single textbook, for example, for mathematics or science. There are specific tools and strategies that we can share with young readers to help them learn how to process these texts.

Difficult concepts can be explored before the text is introduced. We can examine specific content words and terms to find ways of connecting to and understanding them, such as constructing a semantic map. It may be helpful to incorporate visual diagrams, tapes and videos as preparation or as additional support. We can draw attention to the table of contents, to maps and diagrams, and to illustrations. It may help to demonstrate with a simple example of a particular kind of information resource, using an overhead transparency to discuss explicitly how it functions, how the information is organized, and what the cues that characterize that type of text are. We can, with the students, examine parts of the text, making notes and summaries that help "unpack" the words. The teacher can read the text aloud, and then have a chart that reveals and outlines its features. After, the students can work in partners to explore and then derive the information that it offers, sharing their results.

Book Talks

Literacy teachers, curriculum instructors, librarians, and even administrators, need to "market" printed resources with youngsters: books we are reading ourselves; magazines and newspaper articles to be shared with student correspondence; information and surveys to be brought to students' attention. Book jackets and promotional material can be displayed on shelves. New books can be shared and excerpts can be read aloud. A bookshelf with new resources should be available and the items changed frequently. Relevant journal articles can be read or distributed, and computer searches and downloads shared and discussed. Student work needs to be published, displayed and read, and not only hidden in notebooks; we can read what others in our classrooms write. Awards for books and writers can be displayed; a bulletin board can be devoted to strange headlines and interesting articles; students can present their own book talks and reviews, alongside "ten-best lists;" websites can include author profiles, reviews, and related background information. Magazine covers can "paper a room" in history and science, and signal that reading matters in this classroom.

Text Sets

We can gather together sets of print resources focused on a curriculum theme, a particular genre, or an author. The materials can represent different reading levels, with a variety of formats and lengths. These multi-texts give students a broader perspective of the issue or theme they are exploring; they can make use of them in their research and exploration. We need to include opportunities for technological resources — websites and downloads of connected information. Students now can recognize the connections to be made with these multi-texts and understand differences in viewpoints, background, style and intent of the writers. For example, novels can be selected in sets of four or five, by author, by theme, or by difficulty. Non-fiction items can be grouped with poetry and fiction to build a wider frame for the inquiry, a true text set.

A set of resources allows students to build their own personal background knowledge by using texts that are appropriate and accessible. Students can then build support structures for their inquiries, enabling them to read more difficult texts, and to widen their frame of how reading can help them learn. They come to realize the value of multi-texts in supporting their own meaning-making. Different resources are organized and structured in different ways, and often the writer's view and the intent of the information will be different. By having a selection of texts, students can find resources that fit their needs and their abilities.

Building a Literacy Community

Because of the complexities of teaching and learning in today's schools, we need to create a collaborative culture that includes everyone on a school literacy team. We have to develop methodologies and practices in the area of literacy, common across the curriculum, to be used in all classrooms, and share them among other team members, including parents, as we work toward our collective goal of improving literacy with all students.

The most promising strategy for sustained, substantive school improvement is developing the ability of school personnel to function as professional learning communities. As Michael Fullan, an authority on school change, observes, in professional learning communities, "You cannot have students as continuous learners and effective collaborators, without teachers having the same characteristics."

Students now can recognize the connections to be made with these multi-texts.

The most promising strategy for sustained, substantive school improvement is developing the ability of school personnel to function as professional learning communities.

Organizational capacity to boost student literacy and learning in general depends on teachers having shared purposes, collaborative activity to support student success in all subject areas, and the assumption of collective responsibility for students' progress by all the staff.

Many factors affect student success, including family involvement, dealing with issues of poverty, and challenging and effective curriculum. However, the single most influential school-based resource is the teacher. Teachers have a cumulative impact on student achievement. Students develop their literacy skills and they learn to be thinkers, problem-solvers and creators of new ideas when there are reflective, self-directed, interdependent professionals, educators who regularly examine their own practices to ensure ever higher student achievement. In other words, when we can gather, interpret and build understanding based on information we collect and share easily and consistently, we have a real chance to help all students learn more and learn better.

Creating a Culture of Literacy Change

We face several challenges in schools today: test scores rise and fall, and school results in many districts are compared; the literacy difficulties of certain groups of students, often boys, increase; needed technology initiatives are hard to implement without jeopardizing the budget for other resources; class sizes increase; parent concerns are more pressing; and resources for special-needs students shrink. But, there are many teachers, schools and districts pioneering new literacy programs based on solid research. Their successes offer other school communities inspiration as they rethink and develop their own plans for implementing an effective reading and writing curriculum for all students.

There are ways of creating school communities where literacy is at the centre of the curriculum:

- Everyone can participate collaboratively in the process. Administrators, teachers, students, parents and support staff need to forge a common understanding about the goals they hope to achieve.
- School members work together as a team to examine teaching practices, explore new ideas, set priorities, establish shared goals, decide on tasks and determine who will complete them.
- A school staff with a shared vision of what is possible and even achievable can help prepare the members of the team for the difficult times when they may need to modify and even alter plans for implementing literacy initiatives.

- All members of the team are stakeholders in the success of literacy initiatives, and they should receive credit for their efforts. A collective effort to create literacy-based school change is far more effective than a leader imposing his or her ideas on the staff.

In creating a literate school community, all staff need to become researchers, making use of our own experiences, as well as evidence in reports, surveys, professional articles and books, to gather ideas and data that can be analyzed in our own circumstances. Data are our friends; they provide information not condemnation and, like good friends, they sometimes tell us things we don't want to hear even though we need to listen in order to improve. Making decisions about literacy initiatives then rests on interpreting the data in the context of the particular school. Everyone can contribute to the collection of data, to the interpretation of the meaning of the results, and to the formulation of action plans which will be implemented.

> *We continue to grow as professionals through our teaching lives.*

Jennifer Rowsell in *The Literacy Principal* asks: How can schools change their infrastructure and classroom programs to improve student literacy achievement? With a strong literacy initiative in place, how can schools move forward? What can school leaders working with all members of the professional learning community do to bring about such changes?

Success in literacy can ensure success in all curriculum areas, for if students can read, write and talk effectively, they can participate more fully in other areas of learning. We lay the groundwork for effective literacy initiatives when we create a school culture that:

- works as a professional learning community;
- has a strong coherent vision;
- allocates resources appropriately;
- monitors progress;
- takes appropriate action to support initiatives that will make a difference.

The way to improve literacy skills for all our students is not a mystery. As Mike Schmoker puts it, "Incremental even dramatic improvement is not only possible but probable under the right conditions."

Effective Literacy Teachers

In order to create literacy-enriched schools, teachers need to have the craft knowledge and the professional judgment to choose effective teaching and assessment strategies. We need to read professionally, online and in books and journals, to engage in meaningful conversations with our colleagues about the texts we are sharing, to welcome significant changes as professionals, and to feel connected to all of those who share their lives with students. If we read about the teaching of others involved in promising practices, we will find our own programs changing and our professional selves developing alongside others who want to grow as educators.

As teachers, we need to be literacy learners ourselves, in both our personal and professional lives. We may need to uncover our assumptions about how students develop their abilities as readers and writers, and why some have so many difficulties in achieving these goals. Fortunately, we have access to professional resources that can inform and strengthen our knowledge base and our repertoire of useful instructional strategies. We can engage in conversations within professional communities, with our colleagues in school, in online conferences with teachers and educators, in courses designed for us as literacy educators, as members of joint research projects with other teachers and consultants, as attendees at conferences both locally and nationally, as readers of journals and books (electronic and paper) that support and extend successful practices in literacy education, and as members of online professional discussion groups.

We need allies in doing the most for these students with literacy problems.

We want our teaching decisions to be based on our teaching experiences, our careful reflections about our interactions with our students, and relevant and significant insights we gain from our own inquiries and analysis of data. We need to value change, as long as it leads toward more effective teaching and learning in our daily work. We continue to grow as professionals throughout our teaching lives.

Creating Support Networks for Teachers

We need allies in doing the most for these students with literacy problems. If there are school staff members assigned to supportive roles, welcome them to your classroom and offer to work with them in designing a richly integrated program that works for both you and the students. Wherever possible, include them in planning sessions within your classroom community. If students are withdrawn from the class, reorganize the schedule so that the young-sters are gaining, not missing, other meaningful learning experiences. Make use of volunteers who can read aloud to individuals or groups, listen to a student read aloud stories they have written, give book talks, and publish students' writing. You can determine and establish the framework, and volunteers can support its implementation. Enlist the librarian's help in supplying suitable books and online resources. Work with colleagues in your grade division or across levels, developing clear school-wide goals to ensure a continuous program of instruction for those students who will need support throughout their school years. Share ideas with other teachers, and follow the students' progress from year to year. Make it a school policy to provide guidance for each student for the whole of the student's school life.

We need to involve parents wherever possible, without adding guilt or stress to their lives.

Parents as Educational Partners

We need to develop collaborative goals for working alongside the parents of our students. We can discover a great deal about the family literacy in their homes and incorporate that knowledge into the programs we develop for their children. We can increase communication by interviews, phone calls, classroom newsletters, and invitations to parents to visit the classroom, so that parents are aware of how our program functions and can give appropriate support. We can discuss how to assist a troubled reader, why a child needs to read a book silently before sharing it aloud, how to chat with their child about his or her reading and writing, how to find a quiet time for reading, how to extend the range of literacy events in the family setting with TV guides or by writing weekly menus, and how to use the classroom and public libraries to locate books to read aloud (perhaps read by a babysitter or an older sibling). We need to involve parents wherever possible, without adding guilt or stress to their lives, in all aspects of their child's literacy progress, while remembering that they are not teachers, and that the reading and writing experiences at home should be natural and positive so that these students can be helped to work through their difficulties, not punished. Homework is often a troubling time for these students — we need to be aware of the demands we place on these students, and offer parents specific and clear suggestions toward understanding what is necessary to be achieved each night, and how those tasks will support the student's growth as a reader and a writer. We need to value parents as partners in the education of their children.

Difficulties can arise when parents do not know about the school's philosophy of literacy teaching — therefore, teachers need to constantly inform parents about the strategies they are using and provide careful documentation of each student's growth. Parents need to understand how literacy is the basis of the curriculum, so that when they see their children reading silently and aloud, revising, explaining and researching, they will know that their children are learning about language as they work with it.

When parents see teachers' plans — with long-range goals set out — and observe careful records of students' progress, they will grant teachers the support they need to make a curriculum based on the students' own language development success. Effective school leaders recognize the strengths of a solid relationship with the community in building significant literacy programs.

Cooperation between parents and teachers in students' learning is a comparatively new field, although the research findings and examples of good practice are accumulating. Parents are their children's first teachers. As keen observers of their children's development and emerging personalities, they can offer insights into what might help their children learn better in the classroom. In addition, if parents have a clear understanding of the expectations of the curriculum, they can extend and enhance what students learn in school. We need to move away from the traditional split between home and school and toward a genuine sharing of responsibility for children's education. Whatever the future holds, we are now convinced that parents must be included as partners in their children's learning.

Students need to be helped to understand their own learning strengths and weaknesses

When students understand their learning challenges and are supported by caring parents and teachers, they can ask for the help they need and make steady progress. This student was able to make meaning from the cues in the environment and she was reinforced in her efforts by parents who took things one step at a time with her and sought appropriate instructional support for her through tutoring and specialized extra programs. Tanya was helped to understand her own learning strengths and needs and was able to act as her own advocate in the secondary school classroom to ensure that she was given the assistance she required to succeed.

Name of Student: Tanya
Grade or Age: Grade 7
By: Miriam John

Tanya, although a bright, enthusiastic, and eager student, was still not learning how to read print. After the test results came in, her parents decided to enroll her in a private school with a Special Education stream beginning in grade 2. The classes were geared towards language-based learning disabilities and had a maximum of seven children in each class. Among Tanya's challenges was short-term memory processing. Tanya loved her new school and she found the environment very supportive, but she really struggled in all academic areas.

Happily for her, her parents and teachers recognized that Tanya was an extremely intuitive and observant child and quite skilled at making meaning from stories and books and from the world around her. Instead of forcing her to read an entire novel herself, a task that would have been arduous and pointless, they would read to her, occasionally having her read a page or two.

In grade 6, she still found reading print so difficult that she couldn't keep up with the workload on her own. She was working and trying so hard and it didn't seem to be doing any good. Tanya's mother worked with the school to begin a one-on-one remedial reading program in the hope of helping her achieve greater fluency and confidence. She also began looking for other resources to help Tanya. The summer after grade 7, Tanya went to a summer program at a school outside of the district specifically for children with language-based learning disabilities.

Tanya's ability to read print text "took off" that summer. Whether it was the program, Tanya's hard work, or the fact that everything just finally came together for her is hard to determine, but Tanya's reading improved greatly. She sailed through grade 8 and spent another summer at that special program.

Tanya still struggles and still has to work very hard, but she is currently in a regular grade 9 program, following the regular grade 9 curriculum, with modified expectations, with the help of a tutor. At one time, no one ever thought would be possible for Tanya.

Tanya knows a great deal about herself as a learner, which she is now able to articulate in order to help find strategies that will help her. A story about a grade 9 science teacher who was not particularly understanding of her learning style and who was not making any modifications for her illustrates this point. Tanya was getting a failing grade and the teacher even made her redo an assignment. Instead of waiting for her parents to get involved, Tanya took the initiative, went to the teacher, and explained her learning challenges and needs to him. He agreed to read the questions to her for the next test — and Tanya got 91%!

Judy Martin
- Primary teacher with experience in the Intermediate Division
- Galileo Educational Network Association
- Taught most recently at Banded Peak School, Bragg Creek, Alberta

"I don't believe in a deficit model. I learned that from my mother, who was in a coma for two years and we were told she could never walk or talk again. If we had focused on her deficits, she wouldn't be speaking, walking and driving today. I work from an enhancement perspective, and for me, the word **'can't'** really means **'children who need more time.'**"

Literacy strategies that work

- use portfolios to enable students to identify strengths and areas for improvement, and to allow them to work in a self-directed way;
- give students an audience greater than the teacher and a purpose for reading and writing;
- support inquiry through projects on real-life issues (e.g., extinction and endangered animals);
- use online experts in the field explored in order to help students open up the widest possible window of inquiry;
- develop writing from the questions and ideas students are exploring;
- use material that interests students and give them authentic answers to their questions based on this in order to increase their reading level. Students will be motivated to read the answers to determine where their next steps will be.
- teach skills missed in operation in order to move to the next level, never as isolated exercises;
- move things forward to the next level of inquiry from students' point of understanding, scaffolded by the teacher's feedback ;
- sustain and expand student interest, and provide a real need for exploring vocabulary, by having someone "in the real world" respond to student work;
- use technology, along with writing buddies (often older students), for editing.

Assessment:
- use assessment to document students' progress toward clearly articulated goals;
- look at the work of the children, rather than the creation of lessons and activities in isolation;
- work on difficulties in the context of the work students have produced;
- examine students' work with them to ask the question: "What do you need to work on next?"
- create rubrics using the Inquiry Online environment, an inquiry-based program of planning that goes through specific steps with an online component. This allows contact with other teachers in order to develop the tasks for specific projects on which students are working;
- create rubrics specifically for tasks;
- have students understand and help determine how their work will be evaluated;
- differentiate based on students' needs;
- use ongoing daily classroom assessments to determine the next steps for learning and teaching;
- see large-scale assessment as another piece of information about performance;
- use examinations and tests in order to show what students have learned;
- build on what needs to be done, rather than try to "fix" weaknesses with a recovery program; do not use a deficit model.

Professional Perspectives

CHAPTER 8

Assessment for Learning: How Are We Doing?

> *Sometimes teachers feel they live in the eye of the storm where the challenges are acute and the demands high.*

"Literacy is about more than reading and writing—it is about how we communicate in society. It is about social practices and relationships, about knowledge, language and culture"(UNESCO). Ensuring that our students become broadly literate is critically important to society as a whole. If, in the past, students were able to make their way in the world without the benefit of being fully and dynamically literate, those days are gone forever. Looking ahead, the "haves" and "have-nots" in our society will be determined, more than ever, by their success or failure in becoming literate, and by their ability to keep on learning throughout their lifetimes. To put it starkly, the consequences of students failing at school and not becoming fully literate are more serious than in the past. Students risk being left behind and left out of those important social and economic interactions which provide independence and the capacity to contribute as involved and productive citizens, and fulfilled individuals.

Today, school improvement and high achievement for all students preoccupy everyone involved in education, whether as a policy maker, educator, parent, student or citizen interested in the welfare of communities. Around the world, the job of educators in the 21st century is huge, complex, and critical. Sometimes teachers feel they live in the eye of the storm where the challenges are acute and the demands high. Never has scrutiny of the effectiveness of public schooling and its impact on the quality of life been more intense.

In North America and in many other places around the world, the context in which educators work and live is profoundly different from what it was twenty, ten or even five years ago. The parents in our communities and the students in our classrooms are more informed, more involved, more skeptical about accepted wisdom, more questioning of authority, and more intolerant of ambiguity. More is expected from our teachers and our schools than ever before.

From the outset, we must acknowledge that students want and need to know how well they are doing as readers and writers, where they stand, and what they need to do in order to improve. Teachers need informed and timely feedback on how their students are doing and on which teaching practices are working well. Parents need to be aware of the curriculum mandated and the standards expected in our schools. They need specific information about their children's performance and progress. Citizens need evidence that education of a consistently high quality is available in all schools, and that resources are being used effectively to maximize student literacy learning.

Many able and conscientious classroom teachers keenly feel the need for a clear sense of direction in classroom literacy assessment. They want to identify practices that lead to sustained and dynamic learner engagement. A surprising number of teachers are unsure about how to measure the extent to which their students are meeting the standards or, for that matter, how the standards themselves could best be developed. The philosopher George Kelly summed up the challenge facing education reformers when he wrote that "We need a technology to implement our humane intentions." In other words, how can we ground successful practice in the real lives of students and teachers?

Clearly, good assessment that provides a window on the literacy/learning process is vital. The challenge for teachers is to create a culture of assessment in the classroom that encourages student self-reflection and provides timely and clear information for better decision-making about teaching and learning without becoming "a slow stain that discolours the enterprise" and distracts us from our twin commitments to excellence and equity.

Insights from Assessment

Students themselves are often a source of keen insight, as the following story of a visit to an elementary school with a strong language arts program demonstrates. The program in this school stressed solid literacy practices, keyed to each child's experience. One day, two boys, both about nine years old, were waiting to see the principal so that they could show her some written work, as they were encouraged to do. They weren't in any trouble so they were relaxed, and as they waited, they became very interested in a terrarium the principal kept in the waiting room. They were especially fascinated by the frogs living inside. As they talked about the frogs and pointed at them, one of the boys reached in to pick one up. The other boy exclaimed, "Don't touch that frog or they'll make you write something about it!" There, in short, is the dilemma of capturing students' intentions and motivations without creating artificial contexts which, often unwittingly, discourage real engagement and connection for the students.

Learning through literacy is a complicated process of acquiring the information, skills and capacity to move with confidence and competence from one text to another. It depends on many factors: prior learning, student motivation, student abilities, student engagement with school work, parental attitudes, resources available, and, very importantly, the quality of instruction and the insights from assessment of progress along the way. No one knows the students' emerging competencies as language users, or can figure out all the nuances and specificity of what needs to be done to help students progress, better than the teacher. It is the teacher who is familiar with the expectations for each student's performance and the realities of classroom practice.

> *"Don't touch that frog or they'll make you write something about it!"*

As Rick Stiggins observes, teachers who gather accurate information about student literacy achievement through the use of sound classroom assessment contribute to effective teaching and learning. On the other hand, those who fail to understand and apply the insights and evidence for sound assessment risk doing great harm to students.

Helping the students improve their literacy skills depends on assessment tasks that illuminate the characteristics of exemplary reading and writing. These tasks can provide helpful direction to students as they work to improve their own performance. Grant Wiggins says assessment should be "educative" in two essential ways.

"First, assessment should be deliberately designed to teach (not just to measure) by revealing to students what worthy work looks like (offering them authentic tasks). Second, assessment should provide rich and useful feedback to all students and to their teachers... Educative assessment implies that teaching sets possibilities in motion; the quality of the assessment (the challenge set, the feedback obtained, and the adjustments made) and the quality of the coaching will determine how far students will take those possibilities. Achievement depends on the learner attempting, through successive approximations (based on many performance-feedback-guidance cycles), to match or even exceed model performance. Think of being coached in chess or basketball, or recall efforts at losing weight: the 'teaching' is meaningless unless we learn to internalize the methods, insights, and standards through the feedback from results of our attempted performances and through the coach's targeted guidance."

When a group of students in elementary schools in a large jurisdiction were recently polled on the question, "What would make schools better for you?", an eight-year-old third grade student gave an answer that would rival any academic analysis of the question: "You could make schools better if you show us what good work looks like and help us see what comes next."

Assessment Literacy

Michael Fullan describes "assessment literacy" as the ability and the desire to look at achievement data, to share results, to get more knowledgeable and to improve instruction. Strong and enlightened assessment and evaluation practices in every classroom are critical to schools working as learning communities to ensure all students join the literacy club, regardless of the challenges they face.

In order to help all our students achieve high levels of literacy, we need to be sure the following guidelines are in place in our schools:

1. Teachers monitor all aspects of language in use, with multiple measures, and provide wide and varied opportunities for students to demonstrate their reading and writing abilities.
2. Students are given the opportunity and skills to evaluate their own reading and writing, so that they can monitor their progress and set realistic goals.
3. Parents and the broader school community have opportunities to provide a supportive, informed environment that encourages and extends students' ongoing literacy growth.

> *"You could make schools better if you show us what good work looks like and help us see what comes next."*

> "Assessment of learning is assessment for accountability purposes to determine a student's level of performance on a specific task or at the conclusion of a unit of teaching and learning. The information gained from this kind of assessment is often used for reporting. Assessment for learning, on the other hand, acknowledges that assessment should occur as a regular part of teaching and learning, and that information gained from assessment activities can be used to shape the teaching and learning process."
>
> *Assessment for Learning*, Melbourne, Australia

There are no students more in need of this focused attention on their progress, and the appropriate interventions to make learning more successful, than those students who don't, won't, or can't read and write effectively and naturally. The following principles drawn from Britain's Assessment Reform Group outline how assessment for learning should guide classroom practice:

- Literacy assessment should be part of the effective planning for teaching and learning, providing opportunities for both student and teacher to obtain and use information about progress towards meeting reading and writing goals.
- Assessment of students' reading and writing progress should be sensitive and constructive; any assessment has an emotional impact, particularly if students are having difficulty.
- Literacy assessment should focus on how students learn. The process of learning has to be in the minds of the teacher and the student when assessment is planned and evidence is interpreted. Students should be as aware of the "how" of their learning as they are of the "what." This is especially important for struggling learners who often see school as disconnected from their personal lives and experiences.
- Literacy assessment should be recognized as central to classroom practice. Much of what teachers and students do in the classroom can be described as assessment when it involves students demonstrating their knowledge and skills in response to reading, writing and speaking tasks in a wide variety of ways. These assessment practices involve the teachers and learners in discussing and making decisions about next steps in the learning.
- Literacy assessment should be regarded as a key professional skill for

teachers, inextricably interwoven with the development of instructional expertise.

- Literacy assessment should take account of the importance of student motivation, and foster student engagement by emphasizing progress and achievement rather than failure. Comparisons with others who are more successful readers and writers are unlikely to motivate students who are facing challenges. This kind of feedback can also lead to their withdrawing from the learning process in areas where they have been made to feel that they are "no good." Motivation can be preserved and enhanced by assessment methods that protect the student's autonomy, provide some choice, offer constructive feedback, and create opportunity for self-direction.

- Literacy assessment should promote commitment to reading and writing goals, and a shared understanding of the criteria by which they are assessed. Students should receive constructive guidance on how to improve by receiving clear and positively focused information about their reading and writing performances and how to further enhance strengths and tackle problems.

- Literacy assessment develops students' capacities for self-assessment so that they can become reflective, self-managing, independent learners who have the ability to seek out and gain new skills, new knowledge and new understandings.

- Literacy assessment should recognize the full range of achievement of all students. It should enable all learners to achieve their best, demonstrate their reading and writing competencies in a variety of ways, and have their efforts recognized. Students who have many ways to exhibit or demonstrate what they know and can do get hooked on learning and become enthusiastic lifelong learners.

In short, teachers must find the right tools to assess students' reading and writing abilities.

Links Between Assessment and Instruction

It is through classroom assessment that attitudes, skills, knowledge and thinking are fostered, nurtured and accelerated — or stifled. As we reflect on our daily classroom practice, and think about the links between assessment and instruction, it is helpful to consider the following questions:

1. What is the purpose of this literacy lesson/task/unit/program?
2. How will I know if the students understand and have achieved the purpose of the literacy experience?

3. What tasks and contexts should I provide to promote literacy learning and permit students to demonstrate their progress in reading and writing?
4. What are the most appropriate methods for gathering the data/evidence of how students are developing reading and writing skills?
5. What tool(s) should be used to record the data?
6. With whom should data be analyzed? Shared?
7. What conclusions, if any, can be drawn from an analysis of the literacy data?

Good assessment practices imply simultaneously, and, we might add, paradoxically, individualizing and standardizing. Teachers must find the right tools to assess students' reading and writing abilities, evaluate or diagnose their individual progress, and juxtapose this against expectations set out in the curriculum and illustrated by exemplars. Of course, analysis of the information from the assessments taken collectively across the school can provide helpful indications of where new efforts are required. When considering the results of student performances on large-scale district assessments, it is often useful for schools to consider the data on their students achievement in light of the results schools with similar characteristics and populations are achieving. This comparison among "statistical neighbours" can often shed light on which next steps could be taken.

In the end, what is clear from research, theory and practice is that it is important to assess all areas of students' development to improve literacy achievement in each classroom and across the school. To do this, we need to gather data from a variety of sources, as well as communicate with and consult teachers, students and parents, to crystallize what we need to do to create successful literacy-based change.

In what follows, we have highlighted key modes and tools of assessment that have proven successful in indicating a student's literacy progress, including more formal measures of reading and writing development, in order to reinforce our belief in balancing these approaches with daily, weekly and monthly informal approaches in assessing literacy development. Student portfolios can include a variety of examples of student work in literacy.

Observation Guides, and Checklists

Observation guides and checklists are indicators of a student's progress. The key to any effective literacy initiative lies in combining several assessment tools simultaneously, so that no one guide can be viewed as absolute or sufficient.

Checklists and guides are most valuable when they are repeated several times throughout the year. In this way, trends and progress that occur over the year can be noted. For example, in the case of reading, they can help show how a student is developing as a reader – the level of fluency, use of strategies and awareness of cueing systems. Observations arising from checklists can be shared with students, too, to encourage them to take responsibility for their learning by focusing on areas that require change.

A published tool such as Marie Clay's Observation Survey for assessing reading development addresses concepts about print by applying a criterion-referenced approach to reading development and is targeted for emergent literacy learners. The Observation Survey helps students develop independent reading strategies such as cross-checking, self-monitoring and searching for meaning. It also measures letter identification, concepts about print, sight word reading, and hearing and recording sounds in words, oral reading and writing vocabulary.

Anecdotal Records

Anecdotal records are those that teachers keep on an informal basis as they observe students in their day-to-day learning. A teacher may choose to observe students in groups as well as on an individual basis.

Students often provide useful information in reading inventories, and anecdotal recording is one way of keeping track of this information. Inventories, where students complete a list of their achievements, favourite activities, or interests, can be extremely helpful when planning topics for individuals and groups to explore in class. Additionally, inventories can tell a teacher about students' feelings related to aspects of their learning and information that may not be visible in class.

Reading Interviews

A reading interview is a series of open-ended questions designed to discover:
- the strategies used by proficient or inefficient readers;
- how students cope with difficult material;
- which qualities typify "good" readers, according to students;
- which reading strategies students would recommend to others;
- students' personal strengths and weaknesses.

Reading interviews can be conducted in an informal setting, relatively free from interruption. Notations of students' responses can be written or taped. A teacher may wish to conduct reading interviews several times during the year to determine if attitudes have changed and if there has been development in students' knowledge about the process of proficient reading.

Retellings

Employing retelling of a text as a form of assessment promotes a meta-awareness of text content, design and structure. It also facilitates a greater awareness of the variety of texts made available to students over the course of their learning. The retelling procedure causes learners to bring to their conscious awareness many features of text structure on which they would not typically focus, or upon which they would not typically reflect. By sharing retellings with peers, students make explicit what would previously have been primarily implicit, and have the opportunity to apply their previous knowledge and experience to new types of texts.

…entries can take many forms including point-form notes, webs, illustrations and notes to their teachers.

Running Records

The running record, developed by Marie Clay, like miscue analysis, presents a record of a student's reading behaviour on a specific text. In this procedure, a teacher sits beside a student while the student reads a text so that both the teacher and the student are looking at the same text. The student reads a text that she or he has read before, although on occasion, a new text might be read once or twice as a final assessment of progress.

The text should be one that presents some challenges so that the teacher can observe the problem-solving strategies the student is using. However, it should not be so difficult that the student cannot continue to read. If it is, the student cannot put into use the strategies that she or he possesses, resorting to guessing or to sounding words out at the expense of understanding the meaning. As a student is reading, the teacher observes closely. In this way, a teacher acts as an observer rather than an instructor, recording all of the information the student reads. If a student cannot continue because of a difficult word, the teacher can tell the student the word so that the reader can move forward and maintain fluency.

The most common miscues we find in running records are substitutions, omissions, insertions and reversals. They fall broadly into three categories — graphic change, meaning change and structure change. Of these three, those mistakes that result in a change of meaning are most serious, since they reflect a lack of understanding of the text on a student's part. If a student makes mistakes in all three categories, particularly those relating to meaning, and does not self-correct, a teacher can determine that the passage is too advanced for the student.

Reading Conferences

Conferences about reading are an invaluable source of information about students' literacy experiences. In this type of assessment, students bring their literacy portfolios containing their reading journal entries to a conference to discuss their growth as readers with their teachers. Informal discussion questions may relate to the number of books read, the number of books begun but not finished, and the reasons for this. Based on the results of such a conference, a teacher may conduct reading inventories and/or set goals with students (for example, setting a number of pages or books to be read; reading books from another genre, and so on).

However, it should not be so difficult that the student cannot continue to read.

Reading Response Journals

Reading response journals contain students' ideas about, reactions to, and opinions of what they have read. They are a way for students to organize their thoughts and to record ideas generated by a story. When students first use a journal, many simply retell what they have read. As their familiarity grows and their confidence as readers develops, students begin to use their journals as a sounding board for their perceptions and reactions. To achieve this, students need to write in their journals regularly. Their entries can take many forms including point-form notes, webs, illustrations, and notes to their teachers.

The purpose of teachers reading these journals is to discover what students are thinking about in their reading, to help them to develop as readers, and to focus on making meaning. When teachers respond to students' journals, they can comment on the students' ideas and reflections, perhaps making connections between experiences, and encouraging them to explore other aspects of their reading. Teachers can share their own responses to a book.

Cloze Procedures

Cloze procedures involve oral or written deletions of parts of words, whole words, or phrases in a passage of text. "Clozing," or restoring these gaps, requires students to scan the text, recognize and process contextual cues, and then choose the most appropriate word or phrase. In this way, the reader learns to use context to help figure out unfamiliar word, and it is an active and constructive language process.

Cloze activities are suitable for use at all grade levels and can help to build a number of skills exhibited by strong, fluent readers, including:

- focusing on contextual cueing systems;
- anticipating what will happen in the text;
- interacting with text in a variety of ways, such as searching, scanning, and thinking, that can result in making more meaning with print;
- developing a repertoire of thinking strategies;
- gaining confidence in recognizing words;
- increasing the student's comprehension and vocabulary awareness.

> *Profiles can be created at the beginning of the year, to get a general picture of each child's writing behaviours and strategies.*

Profiles of Writing Behaviour

Observation of young writers at work can provide teachers with information about students' knowledge of the skills and processes of writing. A profile of writing is designed to form the basis for in-depth, ongoing observation. It is a record of the kinds of behaviours and methods of working demonstrated by each student. Observers can note which behaviours are evident, and decide whether they are appropriate for the particular task and stage of writing. The observations can later form the basis for discussions with the student, and for reporting to parents or in-school review committees.

Profiles can be created at the beginning of the year to paint a general picture of each student's writing behaviours and strategies. They can then be used at intervals throughout the year to monitor those students whose strategies do not seem to be productive. Profiles might be used as a basis for a sustained observation of one student, or to observe a number of students at five-minute intervals throughout a writing session to see the activities in which students are engaged.

Exemplars as Benchmarks

In response to more structured language curricula, provincial and state governments have produced documents that furnish examples of high and low achievement in reading and writing. Exemplars are intended to serve as models for boards, schools and teachers in setting reading and writing tasks.

As the Ontario Ministry of Education explains, using exemplars over the course of a literacy initiative can help to identify students' reading and writing levels in the following ways as exemplars:

- show characteristics of student work at each level of achievement for each grade;
- promote greater consistency in the assessment of student work from grade to grade and across provinces and states;
- provide an approach to improving student learning by showing students' written work completed at their level;
- offer clear criteria by which to assess students' written work;
- illustrate the connections between what students are expected to learn and how their work can be assessed on the basis of levels of achievement.

Examinations and Tests

Both large-scale assessments, commercially designed or created for district-wide use, and teacher-designed classroom instruments are helpful when assessing learning against clearly defined expectations. If information gleaned from a test or an examination does not reflect a teacher's ongoing assessment data, the testing instrument may need to be reconsidered. A less likely scenario involves the teacher adjusting his or her ongoing assessment of the student's performance. If both the test and instruction are sound, it is important to keep in mind that there are a number of reasons that a student may not perform well on an isolated test, or any assessment for that matter. There might have been a bad night's sleep or a problem at home. Test results should be viewed as only one part of the puzzle.

Anne Davies, in *Making Classroom Assessment Work,* uses the metaphor of assessment as *inukshuks* or "markers of stone" that guide travellers to their destination. In planning your school's literacy initiatives, it is helpful to regard assessment as navigating a course for each student which helps students figure out where they are headed, how to get there, and finally, celebrates their safe arrival.

Using other literacies

Finding a topic where the student can "teach" the teacher something, such as Xavier did with his knowledge of video games, can open the door to writing texts which can serve as reading material for the struggling reader. By working with the student to scribe a story based on the child's authentic understanding of a particular topic, a rich reading text can be generated which helps the student overcome reticence in trying to read because he or she is reading his or her own ideas and words. Drawing on a student's prior knowledge and experience is a key strategy in helping readers make sense of text.

Name of Student: Xavier
Grade or Age: Grade 3
By: Debbie Crozier

Xavier is eight years old, the youngest member of his family. He has three other siblings, all girls, aged 9, 14 and 17. He is closest to his nine-year-old sister. Xavier enjoys playing outside and playing video games. He is not involved in any sports or other extracurricular activities. He has responsibilities at home which include vacuuming, helping with the dishes and keeping his room clean.

All communications with home are through the mother. The father is present in Xavier's home life, but he does not attend school functions or deal with school matters. Xavier is very attached to his mother. The mother stresses the fact that she has a very busy schedule, but she is willing to listen to reports on her son's progress at school. She is aware that his performance at school is consistently below grade level and is open to informal testing to see where his strengths and weaknesses are. The mother is also appreciative of any resource support that can be given at school to her son.

In class, Xavier is very quiet and rarely participates. He needs to be encouraged to participate in his small guided reading group; however, Xavier will freely raise his hand to respond to questions he has completed if he's sure his answers are correct. He is not a risk taker and I feel this is a result of his repeated failure to meet grade level expectations, particularly in math and language. He performs slightly better in basic numeracy. Xavier has been flagged each year by the classroom teacher, and Special Education resource teachers have been involved in planning for his education. Xavier received Reading Recovery™ assistance in grade 1 and exited the program reading at level 17 in the Benchmarks Kit. However, when assessed in early grade 3, he had difficulty reading at level 15. He needs to be encouraged to use various reading strategies and he has poor fluency, which makes comprehension difficult. He has a definite preference for non-fiction over fiction print text.

When I recently sat down with Xavier and told him we'd be writing a story together, he didn't show any emotion; however, he rarely shows emotion. As we brainstormed ideas for the story, I asked him what he likes. At Xavier's silence, I suggested animals, friends, and video games, but there was still no response until I listed various kinds of animals and then video games. When I mentioned Super Mario, Xavier responded, slowly at first but, as he taught me about the video game, I found out he had a lot of knowledge about the game. We had stumbled onto a strong story grammar. My goal is to use this knowledge of the video game to create a story which Xavier will be able to read. We'll start by reading it together, then independently, and finally I'd like him to share it at home.

Identification of Special Needs

Early intervention and appropriate assessment to diagnose learning problems can prevent years of frustration and anxiety. Self-confidence and engagement are seriously jeopardized when students don't receive the focused instructional support that they need early in their schooling in order to prevent discouragement and lost opportunity.

Name of student: Laura
Grade or Age: 23 years old
By: Bianca Auciello

Laura has always been very creative and marched to the beat of her own drummer. As a child, she loved to make up plays and stories, which she would record into her Fischer Price tape recorder. She would do all of the voices and throw in a song or two. She rarely wrote down any of her inspirations because she was a poor speller and, even though she liked to create new worlds and characters in her plays, she disliked reading.

Listening to literature and watching movies were very enjoyable for her, but she never chose to pick up a book on her own. This caused great frustration for her parents, who loved to read and who would often go to the library. At the library, however, Laura would choose books on topics of interest with illustrations, staying away from books with a lot of print text.

When it was time to start school, her parents chose Montessori for her because they thought that she might benefit from an alternative setting. She loved it there, and seemed to be doing very well, but the decision was made eventually to put her into the public school system, fearing she would have difficulty with the more rigorous work in the higher grades.

As she got older, Laura had problems with her school work. She would often fall behind if someone at home did not help her with her work. Her progress in school was not setting off any alarm bells, though, because she was charismatic and participated well. However, when she reached high school, her feelings of being overwhelmed by her work intensified. She couldn't keep up in courses with a lot of reading and independent work. Her parents helped her out as much as possible at home with books on tape, organizational skills, and proofreading writing assignments. Things came to a head for Laura when she started at the University of Toronto. She had tremendous difficulty managing all of her work, and textbooks on tape were much harder to come by. Lectures, as well, were a nightmare as taking notes was a daunting task for Laura.

After many tears, bad grades, speculative diagnoses and threats to drop out, Laura was tested for learning disabilities. It was discovered that she does have learning disabilities that interfere with her ability to process information quickly, manage a lot of tasks at one time, and keep her attention focused on a task for an extended period of time.

With this new information, she was able to seek help from disability services and she decided to study part time. Her school work, reading and writing included, improved tremendously. Laura is currently 23, a University of Toronto graduate, and is now studying interior design at Humber College, where the texts are less focused on print and are more visual and aesthetic. She has a renewed sense of confidence in herself and her abilities.

Helena Butler
Mount Pearl Junior High School
St. John's, Newfoundland

"In order to engage and help students to develop their language ability and confidence, teachers must develop lessons using students' prior learning experiences therefore creating meaningful activities that engage a multiple of intelligences."

"Students benefit from the school board, the school and the community's commitment to a new form of literacy — a form that sees literacy not as something that is acquired, but as something that is done."

Literacy strategies that work

- provide a balanced literacy program through a variety of approaches from teacher-guided reading, to groups thinking critically about text, to independent reading;
- recognize the importance of the visual; have students work through a pop culture unit focusing on a critical analysis of music videos. Students respond to music videos through guided group discussions, role playing and individual journals;
- design a guided-writing program ranging from writing plays to reports for social studies; use group dialogue to help students to compose together using a blackboard, overhead or computer;
- encourage students to express individual tastes and interests through the critical lens of their own diverse backgrounds and circumstances.

Other points to consider:
- encourage students to develop their writing skills and confidence by being pen pals;
- create a Literacy Fair where students share a project or display a response; include in the response various learning styles and all strands of the language process: speaking/listening/reading/writing/representing. Responses should encompass many texts: models, artwork (sketches, paintings, posters, collages, cartoons), costumes, videos, musical performances, poetry, webpages, games, tableaux, scripts, portfolios, and oral presentations;
- set up a book-selling stall to encourage parents to adopt a book or resource for the school library or to purchase a book to increase the volume and frequency of reading and writing at home.

Professional Perspectives

Walter Hammond
Holy Cross Junior High School
St. John's, Newfoundland

"Having students talk and write about their memories and experiences makes students feel as if their learning and personal stories are central to what we do here in this school."

Literacy strategies that work

- provide many opportunities for students to express diverse ideas and opinions which represent their different backgrounds and experiences;
- have a designated time weekly called DEAR, "Drop Everything and Read Time." Everyone in the school drops what he or she is doing and reads. A range of print texts are made available from magazines to poetry, novels, newspapers and comics;
- create formal Literature Circles that meet during lunch where students discuss novels outside the curriculum that are of interest to them;
- combine both text and visual literacy by having students create a memory book. The book, created using a computer, is a part of an interdisciplinary approach, and allows students to share memories and experiences about their learning through diaries, art and photography.

Professional Perspectives

BIBLIOGRAPHY

Allen, Janet. *The Yellow Brick Roads*. Portland, ME: Stenhouse Publishers, 2000.

Angelillo, Janet. *Writing about Reading: From Book Talk to Literacy Essays, Grades 3-8*. Portsmouth, NH: Heinemann, 2003

Assessment for Learning. http://cms.curriculum.edu.au/assessment/whatis.asp Melbourne, Australia.

"Assessment for Learning: 10 Principles." *Assessment Reform Group*. www.assessment-reform-group.org.uk 2000.

Beers, Kylene. *When Kids Can't Read, What Teachers Can Do: A Guide for Teachers 6-12*. Portsmouth, NH: Heinemann, 2003.

Booth, David. *Even Hockey Players Read: Boys, Literacy and Learning*. Markham, ON: Pembroke Publishers, 2002.

Booth, David. *Reading & Writing in the Middle Years*. Markham, ON: Pembroke Publishers, 2001.

Booth, David, and Bob Barton. *Story Works: How Teachers Can Use Shared Stories in the New Curriculum*. Markham, ON: Pembroke Publishers, 2000.

Booth, David, and Jennifer Rowsell. *The Literacy Principal: Leading, Supporting and Assessing Reading and Writing Initiatives*. Markham, ON: Pembroke Publishers, 2002.

"Building Cross Cultural Literacy." *Education Canada*. 44.2 (Spring 2004), Canadian Education Association (CEA). www.cea-ace.ca.

"Classroom Leadership." *Association for Supervision and Curriculum Development (ASCD) Newsletter*. 7.7 (April 2004).

Clay, Marie M. *By Different Paths to Common Outcomes*. Portland, ME: Stenhouse Publishers, 1998.

Clifford, Pat, and Sharon Friesen. "Leadership and the New Literacies." www.galileo.org/research/publications/leadership_new_literacies.

Davies, Anne. *Making Classroom Assessment Work*. Merville, BC: Connections Publishing, 2000.

Earl, Lorna, and J. Bradley Cousins. *Classroom Assessment: Changing the Face; Facing the Change*. Monograph Commissioned by the Ontario Public Teachers Federation, 1995.

Every Child Learns, Every Child Succeeds. Report and recommendations of Alberta's Commission on Learning. October, 2003.

Ferreiro, Emilia. *Past and Present of the Verbs to Read and to Write: Essays on Literacy*. Trans. Mark Fried. Toronto: A Groundwood Book, 2003.

Fly Jones, Beau, Gilbert Valdez, Jeri Nowakowski, and Claudette Rasmussen. *Plugging In: Choosing and Using Educational Technology*. Council for Educational Development and Research. North Central Regional Educational Laboratory, 1995. www.ncrel.org/sdrs/edtalk/toc.htm.

Fountas, Irene, and Gay Su Pinnell. *Guiding Readers and Writers (Grades 3-6) Teaching Comprehension, Genre and Content Literacy*. Portsmouth, NH: Heinemann, 2001.

Galileo Educational Network. www.galileo/org/research.

Gallagher, Kelly. *Reading Reasons: Motivational Mini-lessons for Middle and High School*. Portland, ME: Stenhouse Publishers, 2003.

Gee, James Paul. *What Video Games Have to Teach Us About Learning and Literacy*. London: Palgrave MacMillan, 2003.

Gordon, David T., ed. *The Digital Classroom How Technology Is Changing The Way We Teach and Learn*. Cambridge, MA: The Harvard Education Letter, 2000.

Gordon, Mary. Speech: "Now that the public schools have the brain research on the early years, what are they going to do with it?" The National Association for the Education of Young Children (NAEYC) Conference. Toronto, 1998.

Graves, Donald. *A Fresh Look at Writing*. Portsmouth, NH: Heinemann, 1994.

Harwayne, Shelley. *Going Public: Priorities & Practice at the Manhattan New School*. Portsmouth, NH: Heinemann, 1999.

Hull, Glynda, and Katherine Schultz, eds. *School's Out!: Bridging Out-of-school Literacies with Classroom Practice*. New York: Teachers College Press, 2002.

Jacobsen, Dr. Michele. *Building New Bridges: Technology Integration, Engaged Student Learning, and New Models of Professional Development in Foothills School Division*. University of Calgary. November 2002.

Jobe, Ron, and Mary Dayton-Sakari. *Info-Kids: How to Use Non-fiction to Turn Reluctant Readers into Enthusiastic Learners*. Markham, ON: Pembroke Publishers, 2002.

Kress, Gunther. *Before Writing: Rethinking the Paths to Literacy*. London: Routledge Publishers, 1997.

Kress, Gunther, and Theo Van Leeuwen. *Multimodal Discourse: The Modes and Media of Contemporary Communication*. London: Arnold, 2001.

Learning as a Personal Event: A Brief Introduction to Constructivism. Southwest Educational Development Laboratory: Technology Assistant Program, 1999.

Lewin, Larry, and Betty Jean Shoemaker. *Great Performances*. Baltimore: Association for Supervision and Curriculum Development (ASCD), 1998.

Lyons, Carol A., and Gay Su Pinnell. *Systems for Change in Literacy Education: A Guide to Professional Development*. Portsmouth, NH: Heinemann, 2001.

MacGilchrist, Barbara, Kate Myers and Jane Reed. *The Intelligent School*. London: Paul Chapman Publishing Ltd., 1997.

Mighton, John. *The Myth of Ability*. Toronto: House of Anansi, 2003.

Ontario Knowledge Network for Learning Report to the Ontario Government. December, 2000.

Routman, Regie. *Reading Essentials: The Specifics You Need to Teach Reading Well*. Portsmouth, NH: Heinemann, 2003.

Schmoker, Mike. *Results: The Key to Continuous Improvement*. Association for Supervision and Curriculum Development (ASCD), 1999.

Scott, Ruth McQuirter, and Sharon Siamon. *Spelling: Connecting the Pieces*. Toronto: Gage Learning, 2004.

SEDL Southwest Educational Development Laboratory. www.sedl.org.

Smith, Frank. *Joining the Literacy Club: Further Essays into Education*. Portsmouth, NH: Heinemann, 1987.

"Standards for Technological Literacy." *The International Technological Association*. www.iteawww.org/

Stiggins, Rick. *Student-Involved Classroom Assessment*. Toronto: Prentice-Hall Inc., 1997.

Taylor, Alan R., and Terresita Salve-Tubianosa. *Student Assessment in Canada Improving the Learning Environment Through Effective Evaluation*. Education Research Series. May 2001: #9.

"The Good School." *Education Canada*. 44.3 (Summer 2004), Canadian Education Association (CEA). www.cea-ace.ca.

Think Literacy Cross-Curricular Approaches Grades 7–12. Ontario Ministry of Education. 2003.

Tomlinson, Carol Ann. "Deciding to Teach Them All." *Educational Leadership*. 61.6 (October 2003): 7–11.

Tovani, Cris. *Do I Really Have to Teach Reading?* Portland, ME: Stenhouse Publishers, 2004.

Tovani, Cris. *I Read It, but I Don't Get It*. Portland, ME: Stenhouse Publishers, 2000.

UNESCO. *Statement for the United Nations literacy decade*: 2003 – 2012.

Wiggins, Grant. *Educative Assessment: Designing Assessments to Inform and Improve Student Performance*. San Francisco: Jossey Bass Education Series, 1998.

Wilhelm, Jeffrey D. *Improving Comprehension with Think-Aloud Strategies*. New York: Scholastic Inc., 2001.

Wilhelm, Jeffrey D. *"You Gotta Be the Book": Teaching Engaged and Reflective Reading with Adolescents*. New York: Teachers College Press, 1997.